ROCK
LYRICS & TITLES
TRIVIA QUIZ BOOK

"featuring pop/rock stars
from the mid-1960s"
--(including British Invasion)--

250 ROCK LYRICS QUESTIONS/
250 ROCK TITLES QUESTIONS

*an encyclopedia of rock & roll's
most memorable lyrics

in question/answer format*

by: Presley Love

Published by Hi-Lite Publishing Co.

Copyright © 2015, 2018 by:
Raymond Karelitz
Hi-Lite Publishing Company
Rock-&-Roll Test Prep Hawaii
P.O. Box 6071
Kaneohe, Hawaii 96744

email comments/corrections: <u>rocknrolltriviaquizbook.com</u>
(808) 261-6666

We encourage all readers to listen to your oldies records while perusing this book. However, public performance of most songs is under copyright restriction by ASCAP/BMI; extensive replication of lyrics is restricted under copyright of the writer and/or publisher.

4th EDITION -- Updated Printing: 2019

Love, Presley

ROCK LYRICS & TITLES TRIVIA QUIZ BOOK (1964-1969)
Volume 1 (128 pages)

1. Rock-&-Roll Trivia Quiz Book   I. Love, Presley   II. Title: Rock and Roll

2. Music

COVER DESIGN: *Doug Behrens*

ISBN: 978-1516842599

Printed In The United States of America

A Magical Musical Tour Through the Past

Once you open this book, you will be transported back to the time of magical musical memories, a mosaic of music at your fingertips!

Browse through the streets where the '60s still rule. Test your rock-trivia expertise — invite your friends to see who's the ROCK LYRIC KING!

Rock & Roll is here to stay, and now every memory-making word can be recalled whenever you feel like escaping to the past, groovin' where no person has gone before! Put on your oldies records, let their words of wisdom come alive for you, then sit back in ecstasy and let the good vibrations take you on a magic swirling ship headed on a collision course with the classics!

****

To be best prepared for this memory-making book, listen to lots of rock & roll — heavily energized with the Beatles and the Beach Boys — and be sure not to forget the Motown sound, the British Invasion bands, and even the "Prefab Four"! (For even more added flavor, light a stick of incense and turn on your lava lamp.)
    [caution: a strobe-light may cause '60s flashbacks!]

----

text collection by: **Presley Love**
format/production by: Raymond Karelitz

The Legacy of Presley Love

In 1992, music-aficionado Presley Love compiled a vast treasure of rock and roll lyric-memoribilia, including songs from the earliest days of rock and roll up through the late 1980s. This musical quiz-format collection lay dormant except for the release of one small volume, which contained 400 questions. The original book — printed in 1992 — became, over the years, an Amazon.com favorite, with very positive response from those who loved the book for its "party-flavor" appeal.

In 2014, the entire vault of Presley Love's music-lyric memoribilia was located in a storage locker — containing his collection of lyric-questions and trivia questions in quiz format! After four years of diligent compiling and organizing, the entire Presley Love collection of rock lyrics, rock titles and rock group trivia is now available in quiz-format!

We are proud to unveil the first volume of this rare and collectible series: *ROCK LYRICS & TITLES TRIVIA QUIZ BOOK* (1964-1969). We sincerely hope you enjoy these fabulous rock-favorites in quiz-format, a preview of the exciting treasure trove of rock & roll memories from Presley Love's truly incredible 1955-1989 collection!

ROCK

LYRICS

QUESTIONS

If you're brave enough to test your skills,
here's a simple SCORING CHART:

(questions are worth 1 point each — "Harder Questions" are worth 2 points each . . . If you are able to correctly answer the question/identify the song without the three choices, you receive twice the point value!)

If you score . . .

25+ Points: You probably STILL think it's 1967!
(Check your wardrobe!)

20-24: You probably paid more attention to
rock & roll than books & school!
(Check your report card!)

15-19: There's a lot of rock & roll memories
in your blood!
*(But maybe it's time to buy
a few more rock & roll LPs!)*

10-14: Don't you wish you'd listened more closely
to rock & roll?!
(It's never too late to be hip!)

0-9: Where were YOU when rock began to rule?!
*(Time to get experienced —
run to your music store now!!!)*

(note: all answers are derived from lyrics within the song)

1. In *Have You Seen Your Mother, Baby, Standing in the Shadow?* what are the Rolling Stones glad they helped you do ?
   - a. open your eyes
   - b. reunite
   - c. break free

   ****

2. What did the Swingin' Medallions have a *Double Shot* of ?
   - a. love
   - b. gin
   - c. buckshot

   ****

3. In *Pushin' Too Hard,* the Seeds say that you'd better stop _____.
   - a. telling them what to do
   - b. fooling around
   - c. acting like a big shot

   ****

4. The Monkees say *I Wanna Be Free* as what kind of bird ?
   - a. an eagle
   - b. a vulture
   - c. a bluebird

   ****

5. In the earliest games that the Hollies played with *Carrie-Ann,* what role did they play ?
   - a. janitor
   - b. teacher
   - c. postman

6. According to Jan & Dean in *Ride the Wild Surf,* what are the people all waxed up and ready just waiting for ?

    a. the surf to build up

    b. an excuse to pick a fight

    c. the sun to tan their bodies

****

7. In *Magic Bus,* the Who are so nervous that they just

_____.

    a. mind their own business

    b. sit and smile

    c. bite their nails

****

8. According to Steppenwolf in *Magic Carpet Ride,* what will set you free ?

    a. the magic carpet

    b. the sounds of the music

    c. the fantasy

****

9. In *I Want to Hold Your Hand,* how do the Beatles say they feel when they touch you ?

    a. funny inside

    b. confused

    c. happy

****

10. In *There But For Fortune,* if you show her the country where the bombs had to fall, what will Joan Baez show you ?

    a. the fall-out shelters

    b. a young land

    c. the graves

11. When is it that Peter & Gordon say *I Go To Pieces* ?
   a. whenever they play with scissors
   b. every time their baby passes by
   c. right before tea time

****

12. In *Cry Like A Baby,* when you just walked by them on the street, how did the Box Tops react ?
   a. they didn't say a word as you passed them by
   b. their heart fell to their feet
   c. they were relieved that you didn't cause a scene

****

13. Even though others are trying to break them apart in *Can't You See That She's Mine,* what do the Dave Clark Five say that they will continue to do with their girlfriend — no matter what people may say ?
   a. they'll party the night away
   b. they'll continue to go steady
   c. they'll keep on holding her hand

****

14. In *Love Me Do,* the Beatles want someone to love, somebody _____.
   a. new
   b. true
   c. cute

****

15. *In My Room,* what do the Beach Boys lock out ?
   a. useless chatter and things that don't matter
   b. all the noise in the street
   c. all their worries and their fears

16. According to the 5th Dimension in *Go Where You Wanna Go,* how long have you been gone ?

    a. a week

    b. a month

    c. a year

****

17. Why do the Small Faces say that you can miss school to feed the ducks at *Itchycoo Park* ?

    a. because school's out forever

    b. why go to learn the words of fools

    c. what's better than to learn from nature

****

18. Although they have their girl *Under My Thumb,* what can the Rolling Stones still do ?

    a. look at someone else

    b. still be her best friend

    c. play the guitar without losing a beat

****

19. Though your other boyfriend can buy you furs and diamond bracelets, what can Herman's Hermits give you that is *Just a Little Bit Better* ?

    a. respect and loyalty

    b. their welfare checks

    c. sweet love

****

20. What is it that the Beatles say they don't care too much of because it *Can't Buy Me Love* ?

    a. fancy clothes

    b. foolish promises

    c. money

HARDER QUESTIONS: Worth 2 points each — 4 points if you can answer the question without the three choices!

****

1. Where does Napoleon XIV say *They're Coming to Take Me Away* to ?

> a. the funny farm
> b. the countryside
> c. a secluded island

****

2. Because of all the *Talk Talk*, what can't the Music Machine do ?

> a. go on
> b. make any lasting friends
> c. sleep at night

****

3. In *Yellow Balloon*, where is the Yellow Balloon walking with you ?

> a. in your dreams
> b. in the rain
> c. along the beach

****

4. Where is it that the Monkees want you to *Take a Giant Step* ?

> a. outside your mind
> b. to another place and time
> c. to a fantasy world of dreams

****

5. In *Wear Your Love Like Heaven*, Donovan wants the Lord Allah to kiss him once more and fill him with

_____.

> a. song
> b. love
> c. dreams

ANSWERS

1. a. open your eyes
2. a. love
3. b. fooling around
4. c. a bluebird
5. a. janitor
6. a. the surf to build up
7. b. sit and smile
8. c. the fantasy
9. c. happy
10. b. a young land
11. b. every time their baby passes by
12. b. their heart fell to their feet
13. c. they'll keep on holding her hand
14. a. new
15. c. all their worries and their fears
16. a. a week
17. b. why go to learn the words of fools
18. a. look at someone else
19. c. sweet love
20. c. money

****

HARDER QUESTIONS--Answers

1. a. the funny farm
2. c. sleep at night
3. b. in the rain
4. a. outside your mind
5. a. song

1. In *It's All Over Now,* what is it that the Rolling Stones used to do ?
> a. love her
> b. drink heavily
> c. stay out late at night

****

2. According to Bob Dylan in *The Times They Are A-Changin',* what will happen if the people don't start swimming ?
> a. they'll fall further behind
> b. they'll sink like a stone
> c. there'll be fewer to carry on

****

3. What is it that the Turtles said *You Showed Me* ?
> a. how to find happiness
> b. how to fall in love
> c. how to do the things you do

****

4. In *Did You Ever Have to Make Up Your Mind,* what do the Lovin' Spoonful say happens after you dig a girl the moment you kiss her ?
> a. you find that she has you wrapped around her finger
> b. you start to think how you'll feel when you miss her
> c. you get distracted by her older sister

****

5. According to Jimi Hendrix, what reply does he receive when he asks *Hey Joe* where he's heading ?
> a. up the country
> b. to Mexico
> c. to Gilligan's Island

6. Even though you still want to be just friends with the Supremes in *You Keep Me Hangin' On,* what happens whenever they see you ?

    a. it breaks their heart again

    b. they remember all the good times

    c. they say the silliest things

****

7. In *Dirty Water,* what city do the Standells call home ?

    a. San Francisco

    b. Chicago

    c. Boston

****

8. What is waiting for you and Barbara Lewis if you *Make Me Your Baby* ?

    a. motherhood

    b. paradise

    c. a new tomorrow

****

9. In *Penny Lane,* what do the Beatles say the fireman with an hourglass has in his pocket ?

    a. the keys to his flat

    b. a portrait of the queen

    c. a wallet containing 20 quid

****

10. In *I Fought the Law,* what were the Bobby Fuller Four caught doing ?

    a. smoking in the bathroom

    b. blowing up the high school auditorium

    c. robbing people

11. According to the Rivieras, what are people doing in the warm *California Sun* ?

     a. having fun

     b. getting a tan

     c. groovin' to the music

****

12. In *Don't Worry Baby,* the Beach Boys' girlfriend makes them come alive and makes them want to

    _____.

     a. drive

     b. cry

     c. hide

****

13. According to the Cowsills, why is their *Hair* so long ?

     a. there's no barber shop in town

     b. they don't know why

     c. it's a sign of the times

****

14. Because it's *A Beautiful Morning,* what do the Rascals say it makes no sense to do ?

     a. go to work

     b. wear a frown

     c. stay inside

****

15. In *Till the End of the Day,* when do the Kinks say that they feel good ?

     a. on a sunny afternoon

     b. after a few beers

     c. from the moment they arise

16. In *Homeward Bound,* as they prepare to play a tour of one-night stands, what do Simon and Garfunkel have with them ?
   a. a suitcase and guitar
   b. a bottle of booze
   c. a picture of you

****

17. Gary Lewis & the Playboys say that *This Diamond Ring* can be something beautiful under what condition ?
   a. if there's a girl to give it to
   b. if you pawn it at the perfect time
   c. if there's love behind it

****

18. The Archies call their *Sugar, Sugar* their

  _____.
   a. party animal
   b. candy girl
   c. midnight fantasy

****

19. In *Revolution,* what do the Beatles say when you talk about destruction ?
   a. you can count them out
   b. sometime's there's no other way
   c. it's a new sensation

****

20. According to the Rolling Stones, what will *Not Fade Away* ?
   a. lipstick on their collar
   b. the stains from a broken heart
   c. love that's love

HARDER QUESTIONS: Worth 2 points each — 4 points if you can answer the question without the three choices!

****

1. In *The Ballad of the Green Berets,* although 100 men will test today, how many does SSgt. Barry Sadler say will become members of the elite group?

      a. only one
      b. three
      c. none

****

2. When Chris Montez suggests *Let's Dance,* what three dances does he specifically offer for your selection?

      a. the Twist, Stomp, and Mashed Potato
      b. the Frug, Fly, and Watusi
      c. the Tango, Mambo, and Samba

****

3. Clarence Carter wants you and him to *Slip Away* to a place where you're both _____.

      a. left alone
      b. not known
      c. treated fairly

****

4. In *She's My Girl,* where did the Turtles say they were last night?

      a. at her house
      b. up in the sky
      c. painting the town red

****

5. In *Psychotic Reaction,* how do the Count Five feel?

      a. depressed
      b. out of their mind
      c. high as a kite

ANSWERS

****

1. a. love her
2. b. they'll sink like a stone
3. c. how to do the things you do
4. c. you get distracted by her older sister
5. b. to Mexico
6. a. it breaks their heart again
7. c. Boston
8. b. paradise
9. b. a portrait of the queen
10. c. robbing people
11. a. having fun
12. a. drive
13. b. they don't know why
14. c. stay inside
15. c. from the moment they arise
16. a. a suitcase and guitar
17. c. if there's love behind it
18. b. candy girl
19. a. you can count them out
20. c. love that's love

****

HARDER QUESTIONS--Answers

1. b. three
2. a. the Twist, Stomp, and Mashed Potato
3. b. not known
4. b. up in the sky
5. a. depressed

1. In *Turn! Turn! Turn!* what do the Byrds swear it's not too late for ?
 a. peace
 b. preserving the environment
 c. a new beginning
****

2. Why does Gary Puckett & the Union Gap want the *Young Girl* to get out of there ?
 a. because she was never invited
 b. because they may change their mind
 c. because their wife is due home anytime
****

3. What is the name of Mitch Ryder & the Detroit Wheels' *Devil With a Blue Dress On* ?
 a. Sally
 b. Jenny
 c. Molly
****

4. Since what event have the Dave Clark Five been in *Bits and Pieces* ?
 a. since they met you
 b. since the motorcycle accident
 c. since you left them
****

5. According to Eric Burdon & the Animals, what will the *Sky Pilot* do after the order is given and the soldiers move down the line ?
 a. he'll walk with them and hold their hand
 b. he'll notify their next of kin
 c. he'll stay behind and meditate

6. According to the Beach Boys in *I Can Hear Music,* what is it that they never had ?

     a. a hit song

     b. a love of their own

     c. a chance to show how much they care

****

7. In *Tobacco Road,* where do the Nashville Teens say they were born ?

     a. in a cigarette factory

     b. in a crossfire hurricane

     c. in a barn

****

8. In *Get Back,* where do the Beatles say JoJo's home was ?

     a. Tucson

     b. Albuquerque

     c. San Diego

****

9. What do the Classics IV hope their old girlfriend will find amongst the *Traces* ?

     a. a trace of love still there

     b. a faded photograph

     c. a priceless memory

****

10. In *Dang Me,* what does Roger Miller say they ought to do to him ?

     a. pay him overtime

     b. pay him some mind

     c. hang him

11. According to the Rolling Stones, what do they say *I'm Free* to do ?

      a. stay out as late as they want

      b. anything they want

      c. keep on loving you

****

12. In *Come See About Me,* what have the Supremes given up just for you ?

      a. all their hopes and dreams

      b. their friends

      c. smoking and drinking

****

13. What does Barbara Mason say *Yes, I'm Ready* to do?

      a. leave the past behind

      b. fall in love

      c. move in with you

****

14. In *Red Rubber Ball,* what were all you had to give to the Cyrkle ?

      a. complaints and criticism

      b. handouts and sympathy

      c. stolen minutes of your time

****

15. In *She's Just My Style,* what is it about her that drives Gary Lewis & the Playboys wild ?

      a. everything

      b. her name

      c. the way she moves

16. Since knowing *Susan,* what do the Buckinghams say they have been losing ?

    a. their minds
    b. sleep
    c. all their other friends

****

17. In *Rain on the Roof,* because of the way the rain makes you look, what do the Lovin' Spoonful hope ?

    a. that you'll stay indoors
    b. that it rains some more
    c. that the rain turns to hail

****

18. In *Monday, Monday,* what do the Mamas & the Papas say that Monday morning couldn't guarantee ?

    a. that Monday evening you'd still be there with them
    b. that they'd still have a job at the end of the week
    c. that by Sunday they'd still have enough food to eat

****

19. According to the Hollies in *Stop! Stop! Stop!* what does the dancing girl have on her fingers ?

    a. rings
    b. mirrors
    c. cymbals

****

20. What happened to make the Monkees say *I'm A Believer* ?

    a. they saw her face
    b. they went to church and saw the light
    c. they watched their song hit #1 on the chart

HARDER QUESTIONS: Worth 2 points each — 4 points if you can answer the question without the three choices!

****

1. *In the Year 2525,* in what year do Zager & Evans say that, if God's coming, He may say that it's time for Judgment Day ?

> a. 6565
>
> b. 7510
>
> c. 7575

****

2. How old were Eric Burdon & the Animals when they smoked their first cigarette in *When I Was Young* ?

> a. ten
>
> b. thirteen
>
> c. seventeen

****

3. What kind of hair is it that makes the Barbarians wonder *Are You a Boy or Are You a Girl* ?

> a. hair tied in a ponytail
>
> b. long blond hair
>
> c. dreadlocks

****

4. According to the Tradewinds, when is it that *New York's a Lonely Town* ?

> a. when you're lost and don't know where you're bound
>
> b. when you're down to your last cent
>
> c. when you're the only surfer boy around

****

5. In *Mellow Yellow,* who is Donovan mad about ?

> a. Saffron
>
> b. Daisy
>
> c. Chamomile

ANSWERS

****

1. a. peace
2. b. because they may change their mind
3. c. Molly
4. c. since you left them
5. c. he'll stay behind and meditate
6. b. a love of their own
7. c. in a barn
8. a. Tucson
9. a. a trace of love still there
10. c. hang him
11. b. anything they want
12. b. their friends
13. b. fall in love
14. c. stolen minutes of your time
15. a. everything
16. a. their minds
17. b. that it rains some more
18. a. that Monday evening you'd still be there with them
19. c. cymbals
20. a. they saw her face

****

HARDER QUESTIONS--Answers

1. b. 7510
2. a. ten
3. b. long blond hair
4. c. when you're the only surfer boy around
5. a. Saffron

1. According to the Beach Boys, how fast can their *Little Deuce Coupe* go ?

        a. 100 m.p.h.

        b. 140 m.p.h.

        c. as fast as it wants to go

****

2. In *People Are Strange,* the Doors say that people are wicked _____.

        a. when you're unwanted

        b. when you've just come to a new school

        c. when you're in love

****

3. In *You Don't Have to Say You Love Me,* what does Dusty Springfield say she'll never do ?

        a. ask you for money

        b. tie you down

        c. fall in love with you

****

4. Because, just like a ghost, you've been haunting their dreams in *Spooky,* what do the Classics IV say they'll do on Halloween ?

        a. give you a treat

        b. trick you into kissing them

        c. propose

****

5. In *We Gotta Get Out of This Place,* what words of despair do the Animals' friends tell them ?

        a. there ain't no use in tryin'

        b. you're stuck here forever

        c. nobody buys records anymore

6. According to the Beatles, what doesn't the *Nowhere Man* have — which makes him a bit like you and me?

> a. a happy home
> b. love
> c. a point of view

****

7. In *Paint It Black,* what do the Rolling Stones see a line of that are all painted black?

> a. houses
> b. cars
> c. stones

****

8. In *So You Want to Be a Rock 'n' Roll Star,* what musical instrument do the Byrds say you should learn how to play?

> a. a complete set of drums
> b. a tambourine
> c. an electric guitar

****

9. Although love's as easy as pie, what does Len Barry say in *1-2-3* that is the hard part?

> a. living without love
> b. steps 4-5-6
> c. cleaning up afterwards

****

10. In *Hey Baby (They're Playing Our Song),* what do the Buckinghams want to do?

> a. dance the whole night through
> b. get back together
> c. sing a duet

11. According to the Association, what is *Windy* reaching out to do ?

        a. blow the leaves around

        b. sweep you off your feet

        c. capture a moment

****

12. Herman's Hermits say that *Dandy* can't escape the _____.

        a. truth

        b. law

        c. past

****

13. When was it that Jewel Akens said it's time you learned about *The Birds And the Bees* ?

        a. when he looked into your big brown eyes

        b. when you started acting funny

        c. when you started buzzing around

****

14. In *Dream A Little Dream of Me,* while she's craving your kiss, how long is Mama Cass willing to linger ?

        a. until it's dinner time

        b. until dawn

        c. until the dream is over

****

15. Why do the Searchers have to hide their tears in *Needles and Pins* ?

        a. because crying is a sign of weakness

        b. because love isn't worth crying over

        c. because of all their pride

16. Since you've been gone, the Four Tops say *It's the Same Old Song* but with a _____.
    a. different meaning
    b. slower tempo
    c. happier beat

****

17. After tiring of the status-symbol land of *Pleasant Valley Sunday,* what do the Monkees want ?
    a. a girl to love
    b. a change of scenery
    c. the chance to blow it up and start again

****

18. Why is the Beach Boys' love like the *Warmth of the Sun* ?
    a. because it won't ever die
    b. because it heats up with each passing hour
    c. because they can both burn you

****

19. In *I'll Be Doggone,* Marvin Gaye says that if he caught you running around, what would he be ?
    a. righteously angry
    b. a jealous hound dog
    c. long gone

****

20. In *Shapes of Things,* what do the Yardbirds wonder might happen to them when tomorrow comes ?
    a. Will they be bolder than today?
    b. Will you still love them?
    c. What will be the shape of the world?

HARDER QUESTIONS: Worth 2 points each — 4 points if you can answer the question without the three choices !

****

1. In *Hello, Hello,* what does the Sopwith Camel want to share with you ?

    a. their tangerine
    b. their life
    c. their car

****

2. When is it that Love took out *My Little Red Book* ?

    a. when it seemed that the world was passing them by
    b. the minute that you said goodbye
    c. when Saturday night rolled around

****

3. Although people tell them in *Magic Town* that the streets are paved with gold, how do the Vogues find them ?

    a. filled with stories untold
    b. gray and concrete–cold
    c. green—not from money but from mold

****

4. What does the New Vaudeville Band say about *Winchester Cathedral* ?

    a. it's ringing out words of love
    b. its bells are too loud
    c. it's bringing them down

****

5. According to the Doors, what does the *Wishful, Sinful* crystal water cover everything in ?

    a. swirling stripes of orange and green
    b. shades of grey
    c. blue

ANSWERS

****

1. b. 140 m.p.h.
2. a. when you're unwanted
3. b. tie you down
4. c. propose
5. a. there ain't no use in tryin'
6. c. a point of view
7. b. cars
8. c. an electric guitar
9. a. living without love
10. b. get back together
11. c. capture a moment
12. c. past
13. a. when he looked into your big brown eyes
14. b. until dawn
15. c. because of all their pride
16. a. different meaning
17. b. a change of scenery
18. a. because it won't ever die
19. c. long gone
20. a. Will they be bolder than today?

****

HARDER QUESTIONS--Answers

1. a. their tangerine
2. b. the minute that you said goodbye
3. b. gray and concrete-cold
4. c. it's bringing them down
5. c. blue

1. *On a Carousel,* how do the Hollies get closer to their ladyfriend ?
   - a. by changing horses
   - b. by sending letters
   - c. through midnight confessions

****

2. In *House of the Rising Sun,* what profession was the Animal's mother ?
   - a. tailor
   - b. bar maid
   - c. zookeeper

****

3. What will life be for the Young Rascals when they are *Groovin'* endlessly with you ?
   - a. fabulous
   - b. like a party
   - c. ecstasy

****

4. What does Johnny Cash say about *A Boy Named Sue* ?
   - a. he's 6' 4"
   - b. life's not easy for him
   - c. he's got a lot of friends

****

5. When Glen Campbell left *Galveston,* how old was the girl he left behind ?
   - a. sixteen
   - b. twenty-one
   - c. eight

6. What are Paul Revere & the Raiders *Hungry* for ?

    a. a thick and juicy T-bone steak

    b. a night alone with you

    c. that sweet life

****

7. In *Light My Fire,* what do the Doors claim their love could become ?

    a. a funeral pyre

    b. a raging inferno

    c. front-page news

****

8. In *Put a Little Love in Your Heart,* what does Jackie DeShannon hope will be your guide when you look around at the world ?

    a. patience

    b. urgency

    c. kindness

****

9. What are the Four Tops *Standing in the Shadows of Love* getting ready for ?

    a. the uninviting night

    b. a chance to fall in love

    c. the heartaches to come

****

10. In *Respect,* Aretha Franklin admits that your kisses are sweeter than honey, but what else does she say is also sweeter than honey ?

    a. her money

    b. her lips

    c. your lovin'

11. In *This Guy's In Love With You,* what has Herb Alpert overheard regarding your feelings for him?

     a. you think he's shy
     b. you think he's cute
     c. you think he's fine

****

12. What do the Beach Boys say happens when you *Catch a Wave* ?

     a. you lose sight of tomorrow
     b. you can't be beat
     c. you're sitting on top of the world

****

13. In *Something Stupid,* what words do Frank & Nancy Sinatra say that always spoils the evening ?

     a. I love you
     b. give me the bill
     c. it's time to go home

****

14. What is the name of Johnny Rivers' young friend in *Memphis* ?

     a. Annie
     b. Marie
     c. Joanie

****

15. In *Get Off of My Cloud,* when a man visits the Rolling Stones at their apartment, what is he dressed up like ?

     a. a Union Jack
     b. Mister Magoo
     c. a Rolling Stone

16. In *People,* what does Barbra Streisand say about lovers ?
>   a. they're one letter away from being losers
>   b. there are too many of them around
>   c. they're the luckiest people in the world

****

17. Although Neil Diamond's *Cherry Cherry* loves him, when is he going to show her how he feels about her ?
>   a. tonight
>   b. not until he's good-and-ready
>   c. when he's far far away

****

18. Dobie Gray says that when you're with the *In-Crowd,* it's easy to find _____.
>   a. drugs
>   b. romance
>   c. kicks

****

19. In *I Say a Little Prayer,* living without you would mean what to Dionne Warwick ?
>   a. a wish come true
>   b. heartbreak
>   c. loneliness

****

20. In *Lightnin' Strikes,* what does Lou Christie see waiting for him and his girlfriend ?
>   a. a chapel
>   b. stormy weather
>   c. a new direction

HARDER QUESTIONS: Worth 2 points each — 4 points if you can answer the question without the three choices!
****

1. In *Bottle of Wine*, where do the Fireballs want to go ?
   - a. to a bar
   - b. home
   - c. to your house
****

2. In *I Couldn't Live Without Your Love*, what did Petula Clark think of you when she first met you ?
   - a. she didn't like you
   - b. she fell in love with you at first sight
   - c. she didn't know if you'd even notice her
****

3. Where do the Kinks say the *Dedicated Follower of Fashion* does his shopping ?
   - a. at Knightsbridge
   - b. in London boutiques
   - c. in retro shops and underground stops
****

4. In *Liar, Liar,* the Castaways say that there'll come a day when _____.
   - a. it will snow in Honolulu
   - b. you'll be sorry for the things you said
   - c. they'll be gone
****

5. In *Baby, The Rain Must Fall,* what leads Glenn Yarbrough to where he must go ?
   - a. his heart
   - b. his job
   - c. destiny

ANSWERS

****

1. a. by changing horses
2. a. tailor
3. c. ecstasy
4. b. life's not easy for him
5. b. twenty-one
6. c. that sweet life
7. a. a funeral pyre
8. c. kindness
9. c. the heartaches to come
10. a. her money
11. c. you think he's fine
12. c. you're sitting on top of the world
13. a. I love you
14. b. Marie
15. a. a Union Jack
16. c. they're the luckiest people in the world
17. a. tonight
18. b. romance
19. b. heartbreak
20. a. a chapel

****

HARDER QUESTIONS--Answers

1. b. home
2. a. she didn't like you
3. b. in London boutiques
4. c. they'll be gone
5. a. his heart

1. In *Be True to Your School,* what sports did the Beach Boys play in high school ?
    a. baseball and soccer
    b. tennis and bowling
    c. football and track

****

2. What does Tommy Roe say that one day people will be able to say in *Hooray for Hazel* ?
    a. that love is the only answer
    b. that she knows how to cry
    c. that Hazel is a winner

****

3. According to Eric Burdon & the Animals, people of which occupation feel unusually comfortable, warm and at peace in *San Franciscan Nights* ?
    a. businessmen
    b. politicians
    c. policemen

****

4. In *Mountain of Love,* why does Johnny Rivers say that you should be ashamed ?
  a. because you made the mountains crumble to the sea
  b. because you cheated and you lied
  c. because you just changed your name

****

5. According to Matt Monro, when one is *Born Free* what is life good for ?
    a. living
    b. nothing
    c. falling in love

6. In *Daydream Believer,* what time does the alarm awaken the Monkees ?

      a. seven o'clock

      b. six o'clock

      c. noon

****

7. How does *Mony Mony* make Tommy James & the Shondells feel ?

      a. young at heart

      b. so good

      c. hungry for love

****

8. Who must have sent *Your Precious Love,* according to Marvin Gaye & Tammi Terrell ?

      a. heaven

      b. the United States Mint

      c. an angel

****

9. In *Green Grass,* while the bluebirds sing their magic song, what will Gary Lewis & the Playboys do all summer long ?

      a. make love

      b. sing along

      c. sit alone and wonder

****

10. In *It's Your Thing,* how do the Isley Brothers respond to you if you want them to love you ?

      a. that it's no big deal

      b. any time, any place

      c. they've got better things to do with their time

11. According to the Mamas & the Papas, what won't *Words of Love* do anymore ?

  a. pay the bills

  b. replace deeds and actions

  c. win a girl's heart

****

12. In *Come a Little Bit Closer,* what kind of man does the barmaid say Jay & the Americans are ?

  a. a typical American

  b. the kind she could love

  c. so big and so strong

****

13. In *Come Back When You Grow Up,* in what kind of world does Bobby Vee say you're still living ?

  a. in a teenage wonderland

  b. in a fantasy world

  c. in a paper–doll world

****

14. According to Donovan in *Colors,* what is the time he loves the best ?

  a. the morning

  b. sunset

  c. the midnight hour

****

15. If you're without love, what do the Walker Brothers say will also happen as *The Sun Ain't Gonna Shine Anymore* ?

  a. the plants aren't going to grow way up high

  b. the moon isn't going to rise in the sky

  c. there'll be no more ways to get high

16. In *Heart Full of Soul,* how long do the Yardbirds say she's been gone ?
    a. a month or more
    b. for an eternity
    c. a long time

****

17. According to the Fortunes in *You've Got Your Troubles,* what do they and their beleaguered friend both need ?
    a. sympathy
    b. a warm meal
    c. a loving home

****

18. In *Time Is On My Side,* what is it that the Rolling Stones say you're always telling them that you want to be ?
    a. loved
    b. blonde
    c. free

****

19. What reason does the Beatles' girlfriend give to explain why she has purchased a *Ticket to Ride* ?
    a. she could never be free when they were around
    b. other obligations are taking her away
    c. her school starts next week

****

20. In *Ruby (Don't Take Your Love to Town),* how does Kenny Rogers describe his legs ?
    a. as sexy and inviting
    b. as bent and paralyzed
    c. as travel-worn with time

HARDER QUESTIONS: Worth 2 points each — 4 points if you can answer the question without the three choices!

****

1. In what city did Archie Bell & the Drells say they've just started a new dance called *Tighten Up* ?
   - a. Spokane
   - b. Pittsburg
   - c. Houston

****

2. In *Time Has Come Today*, why don't the Chambers Brothers care about what others say ?
   - a. because others say that they don't listen anyway
   - b. because in time they know they'll get their way
   - c. because it'll be gone tomorrow what they say today

****

3. After finding that Aretha Franklin is just a link in your *Chain of Fools*, what does her father tell her to do ?
   - a. come home
   - b. break the chain
   - c. take it in stride

****

4. In *Him Or Me—What's It Gonna Be*, what can Paul Revere & the Raiders still recall you telling them ?
   - a. that you would never ever leave them
   - b. that they were everything you looked for in a man
   - c. that you were only interested in playing the field

****

5. What do the Animals want to do as long as you *Don't Bring Me Down* ?
   - a. be your only boyfriend
   - b. provide for you
   - c. make you feel high

ANSWERS

****

1. c. football and track
2. b. that she knows how to cry
3. c. policemen
4. c. because you just changed your name
5. a. living
6. b. six o'clock
7. b. so good
8. a. heaven
9. a. make love
10. a. that it's no big deal
11. c. win a girl's heart
12. c. so big and so strong
13. c. in a paper-doll world
14. a. the morning
15. b. the moon isn't going to rise in the sky
16. c. a long time
17. a. sympathy
18. c. free
19. a. she could never be free when they were around
20. b. as bent and paralyzed

****

HARDER QUESTIONS--Answers

1. c. Houston
2. a. because others say that they don't listen anyway
3. a. come home
4. b. that they were everything you looked for in a man
5. b. provide for you

1. In *Wouldn't It Be Nice,* what do the Beach Boys say happens the more they talk about getting married ?
   a. the less attractive it seems
   b. it only makes it worse to live without it
   c. the more they want to keep talking about it
****

2. Although the Beatles say all their troubles seemed so far away *Yesterday,* how do things look for them now ?
   a. now they can see a bright, sunshiny day
   b. troubles are even further away
   c. troubles are here to stay
****

3. When Barbara Lewis says *Baby I'm Yours* until two and two is three and the mountains crumble to the sea, she really means _____.
   a. until she can no longer see
   b. until eternity
   c. until you don't mean anything to her
****

4. What does Petula Clark say you can do *Downtown* ?
   a. forget all your cares
   b. take the bus to Chinatown
   c. go dancing
****

5. What did the *Western Union* telegram from the Five Americans' girlfriend say to them ?
   a. that she can't wait to have them back in her arms again
   b. that she doesn't care for them anymore
   c. that they can't keep meeting each other this way

6. In *Stop! In the Name of Love*, what do the Supremes say they know when they watch you walking down the street ?

      a. that you're up to no good

      b. that you've got a bad attitude

      c. that you'll be meeting another girl

7. If you tell them that you'll be their *Woman*, what would Peter & Gordon give up ?

      a. their world

      b. their freedom

      c. their drinking

8. In *Abraham, Martin and John*, what does Dion say seems to happen too often to good people ?

      a. they turn bad

      b. they die young

      c. they become heroes

9. Because he's the *Seventh Son*, what can Johnny Rivers predict ?

      a. the rain

      b. the stock market

      c. the winners and losers

10. What kind of athlete do Jan & Dean say you are when you go *Sidewalk Surfin'* ?

      a. a daring athlete

      b. an asphalt athlete

      c. a pathetic athlete

11. In *Up, Up & Away,* what do the 5th Dimension invite you to do ?
> a. join them in their stoned–soul picnic
> b. take a ride in their balloon
> c. sing their song with them

****

12. *(I'm Not Your) Steppin' Stone,* the Monkees claim that the clothes their girlfriend is wearing are causing _____.
> a. traffic nightmares
> b. the weather to change
> c. public scenes

****

13. Who does Eric Burdon & the Animals say did fly in *Monterey* ?
> a. the Byrds and the Jefferson Airplane
> b. the Grateful Dead
> c. the cops and the hippies

****

14. Among other things, what has Judy Collins looked at from *Both Sides Now* ?
> a. reality
> b. the sun
> c. clouds

****

15. According to Elvis Presley in *Suspicious Minds,* what is he caught in ?
> a. a web of lies
> b. a trap
> c. endless paranoia

16. In *These Eyes*, what do the Guess Who say you did with the promise you gave them ?

        a. you broke it

        b. you gave it away

        c. you forgot all about it

****

17. What couldn't all the people prevent the Who's *Happy Jack* from being ?

        a. gay

        b. carefree

        c. happy

****

18. In *Good Lovin'*, who did the Young Rascals consult regarding their condition ?

        a. the local fortune teller

        b. their family doctor

        c. their ma and pa

****

19. According to the Lovin' Spoonful in *Nashville Cats*, what is it custom-made for any mother's son to be ?

        a. a guitar-picker

        b. unemployed

        c. a tailor

****

20. In *The Boxer*, where did Simon & Garfunkel go as a boy seeking shelter ?

        a. down in the boondocks

        b. to the company of kind strangers

        c. to the poorer quarters

HARDER QUESTIONS: Worth 2 points each — 4 points if you can answer the question without the three choices!
****

1. In *I Feel Free,* how do you move when you dance with Cream ?
   a. like the sea
   b. like a wave out on the ocean
   c. like a bowl of jello
****

2. According to Creedence Clearwater Revival, on what is Poor Boy twanging out the rhythm while he's *Down on the Corner*?
   a. his kazoo
   b. his washboard
   c. his Kalamazoo
****

3. As Donovan was by the sea gazing with tranquility, what did the *Hurdy Gurdy Man* come and do ?
   a. he disturbed everyone's peace of mind
   b. he came singing songs of love
   c. he recited poetry and livened up the scene
****

4. In *A Simple Song of Freedom,* what does Tim Hardin say that people don't want ?
   a. meaningless words in a song
   b. alibis and political lies
   c. war
****

5. Although Billy Joe Royal says *I Knew You When,* he adds that now your love is _____.
   a. stronger than ever
   b. part of someone else's happiness
   c. just a memory

ANSWERS

****

1. b. it only makes it worse to live without it
2. c. troubles are here to stay
3. b. until eternity
4. a. forget all your cares
5. b. that she doesn't care for them anymore
6. c. that you'll be meeting another girl
7. a. their world
8. b. they die young
9. a. the rain
10. b. an asphalt athlete
11. b. take a ride in their balloon
12. c. public scenes
13. a. the Byrds and the Jefferson Airplane
14. c. clouds
15. b. a trap
16. a. you broke it
17. c. happy
18. b. their family doctor
19. a. a guitar-picker
20. c. to the poorer quarters

****

HARDER QUESTIONS--Answers

1. a. like the sea
2. c. his Kalamazoo
3. b. he came singing songs of love
4. c. war
5. c. just a memory

1. In *Jackson*, Nancy Sinatra & Lee Hazlewood got married in a fever that was hotter than _____.
   - a. a peppered sprout
   - b. the blazing sun
   - c. a dog in heat

****

2. What does Stevie Wonder have *For Once In My Life* ?
   - a. a future
   - b. someone who needs him
   - c. joy and happiness

****

3. According to Tommy James & the Shondells in *Crystal Blue Persuasion*, what is the answer ?
   - a. love
   - b. two
   - c. it depends on the question

****

4. According to Steam in *Na Na Hey Hey Kiss Him Goodbye*, your other boyfriend never loved you the way _____.
   - a. they love you
   - b. he should have
   - c. that showed he really cared

****

5. In *Where Did Our Love Go*, now that the Supremes have surrendered themselves to you, what is it you want to do ?
   - a. show them off to all your friends
   - b. marry them
   - c. leave them

6. Who did Neil Diamond, the *Solitary Man,* see holding and loving Jim ?

> a. Melinda
> b. Sue
> c. Johnny

****

7. Because they're so in love *Together,* where do the Intruders say they could be lost and they wouldn't even know it ?

> a. on a desert
> b. in the middle of a jungle
> c. on a barren island

****

8. What place were the Beatles searching for in their *Yellow Submarine* ?

> a. the Land of Oz
> b. the Sea of Green
> c. the Isle of Man

****

9. How does Shirley Bassey describe a kiss from Mr. *Goldfinger* ?

> a. it feels like a million bucks
> b. it's the kiss of death
> c. it will leave you cold

****

10. In *Soul Deep,* what does the Box Tops' love depend on ?

> a. the time of day
> b. the love in your heart
> c. your touch

11. What do the Classics IV say about *Every Day With You Girl* ?

    a. it's only half as good as tomorrow

    b. it's one day closer to the day they'll say "I do"

    c. it's sweeter than the day before

****

12. In *Count Me In,* what do Gary Lewis & the Playboys say you can count them, if they're not first on your list ?

    a. count them out

    b. count them blue

    c. count them pissed

****

13. What time is it that the Rolling Stones say is the perfect time for a *Street Fighting Man* ?

    a. whenever the cause is just

    b. when the sun goes down

    c. summer

****

14. What will the Seekers find in *A World of Our Own* ?

    a. freedom and happiness

    b. peace of mind

    c. the true meaning of love

****

15. In *I Second That Emotion,* what do Smokey Robinson & the Miracles say about a taste of honey ?

    a. it can make a person thirst for more

    b. it's sweeter than wine

    c. it's worse than none at all

16. What is the only thing that *Words* can do for the Bee Gees ?

> a. take your heart away
> b. express their loneliness
> c. bring them happiness in a song

****

17. According to Wayne Fontana & the Mindbenders in *Game of Love,* what did Adam say to Eve in the Garden of Eden ?

> a. baby, you're for me
> b. you've got really nice apples
> c. you're the apple of my eye

****

18. Why do the Beau Brummels say they'll have to die *Just a Little* ?

a. because you're killing them slowly with all your little lies
b. because you won't see them anymore
c. because they have to go away

****

19. According to the Who, what words describe the *Pinball Wizard* ?

> a. rough, tough & good enough
> b. free, wild & nature's child
> c. deaf, dumb & blind

****

20. The Guess Who say there's *No Time* left for

_____.

> a. them
> b. you
> c. anyone

HARDER QUESTIONS: Worth 2 points each — 4 points if you can answer the question without the three choices!

****

1. According to O. C. Smith, if God didn't make the *Little Green Apples,* then where doesn't it rain in the summertime ?

       a. Phoenix
       b. Vancouver
       c. Indianapolis

****

2. In *Can't Find My Way Home,* how does Blind Faith describe themselves ?

       a. as weary and wasted
       b. as lost in an uncertain world
       c. as a cork in the ocean

****

3. In *A Whiter Shade of Pale,* what did Procol Harum do across the floor ?

       a. dance
       b. turn cartwheels
       c. throw a chair

****

4. What happens to make Vikki Carr wish and pray that *It Must Be Him* ?

       a. the doorbell rings
       b. the telephone rings
       c. a voice calls to her in the night

****

5. In *King of the Road,* what is Roger Miller's destination ?

       a. Bangor, Maine
       b. Tucson, Arizona
       c. Naples, Florida

ANSWERS

****

1. a. a peppered sprout
2. b. someone who needs him
3. a. love
4. a. they love you
5. c. leave them
6. a. Melinda
7. a. on a desert
8. b. the Sea of Green
9. b. it's the kiss of death
10. c. your touch
11. c. it's sweeter than the day before
12. b. count them blue
13. c. summer
14. b. peace of mind
15. c. it's worse than none at all
16. a. take your heart away
17. a. baby, you're for me
18. c. because they have to go away
19. c. deaf, dumb & blind
20. b. you

****

HARDER QUESTIONS--Answers

1. c. Indianapolis
2. a. as weary and wasted
3. b. turn cartwheels
4. b. the telephone rings
5. a. Bangor, Maine

1. According to the Beach Boys in *California Girls,* what do the Northern girls do when they kiss ?
   - a. they light up the Southern sky
   - b. they keep their boyfriends warm at night
   - c. they whisper sweet nothin's

****

2. What does Blood, Sweat & Tears say their *Spinning Wheel* hasn't got ?
   - a. an axle
   - b. a home
   - c. a direction

****

3. Why Does Engelbert Humperdinck say to *Release Me* ?
   - a. because he doesn't love you anymore
   - b. because you're cramping his style
   - c. so you can hold him once again

****

4. In *Sure Gonna Miss Her,* what do Gary Lewis & the Playboys call their former girlfriend's new boyfriend ?
   - a. a bird dog
   - b. a lucky guy
   - c. her next victim

****

5. Although he brings the Supremes *Nothing But Heartaches,* what can't they do ?
   - a. break away
   - b. find happiness anywhere else
   - c. get him to leave

6. According to Mercy, *Love (Can Make You Happy)* if you find someone who _____.

     a. likes to swing

     b. is rich

     c. has a love to share

****

7. What does Nilsson say concerning the fact that *Everybody's Talkin'* ?

     a. he can't hear a word they're saying

     b. nobody's listening

     c. nothing is really happening

****

8. According to Richard Harris, what did someone leave out in the rain at *MacArthur Park* ?

     a. the picnic basket

     b. an umbrella

     c. the cake

****

9. Of all the animals alive a long time ago, what do the Irish Rovers say about *The Unicorn* ?

     a. it was the loveliest of them all

     b. it was the loneliest of them all

     c. it was the ugliest of them all

****

10. In *The Last Time,* even though the Rolling Stones say they told their girlfriend once and then twice, what did she never do ?

     a. listen to their advice

     b. melt their heart of ice

     c. cure them of their lice

11. In *Black Is Black,* what color is it for Los Bravos since you've left them ?

  a. black
  b. grey
  c. sunshine blue

****

12. In *Gimme Some Lovin',* why does the Spencer Davis Group say that you'd better take it easy?

  a. because you're about to lose control
  b. because they need to slow down
  c. because the place is hot

****

13. In *Suite: Judy Blue Eyes,* on what days do Crosby, Stills & Nash want you to come see them ?

  a. Tuesdays and Thursdays
  b. Thursdays and Saturdays
  c. Fridays and Saturdays

****

14. At what time does *Gloria* come to Them's house ?

  a. whenever she feels like it
  b. at seven o'clock
  c. around midnight

****

15. The Gentrys urge you to *Keep on Dancing* and

  _____.

  a. romancing
  b. prancing
  c. clapping

16. What does *Wild Thing* do to the Troggs ?
     a. she makes their heart sing
     b. she drives their thing wild
     c. she raises their blood pressure

****

17. When does Marvin Gaye say that *I Heard It Through the Grapevine* ?
     a. today
     b. yesterday
     c. tomorrow

****

18. In *Time of the Season*, what question do the Zombies ask their prospective love-mate ?
     a. Are you lonesome tonight?
     b. Does anybody really know what time it is?
     c. Who's your daddy?

****

19. The Beatles feel that *We Can Work It Out* and get it straight or else say _____.
     a. it's over
     b. what's really on their mind
     c. good night

****

20. In *Daydream*, what do the Lovin' Spoonful say one deserves for being asleep before dawn ?
     a. a medal of courage
     b. a measure of sympathy
     c. a pie in the face

HARDER QUESTIONS: Worth 2 points each — 4 points if you can answer the question without the three choices!

****

1. What is it that the Reflections must find tomorrow to avoid having their love be destroyed by a tragedy *Just Like Romeo and Juliet* ?

    a. the way to your heart

    b. a girl to call their own

    c. a job

****

2. What color were the curtains in Cream's *White Room* ?

    a. black

    b. cream

    c. white

****

3. In *What Now My Love*, Sonny & Cher are watching their dreams turn into _____.

    a. ashes

    b. reality

    c. a television sitcom

****

4. Where did Tommy Roe first meet *Sweet Pea* ?

    a. in a Popeye cartoon

    b. at a dance

    c. in the supermarket

****

5. In *California Nights*, what does Lesley Gore want to do hand-in-hand with you?

    a. walk along the shore

    b. stroll through the park

    c. watch the moon come out

ANSWERS

****

1. b. they keep their boyfriends warm at night
2. b. a home
3. a. because he doesn't love you anymore
4. b. a lucky guy
5. a. break away
6. c. has a love to share
7. a. he can't hear a word they're saying
8. c. the cake
9. a. it was the loveliest of them all
10. a. listen to their advice
11. b. grey
12. c. because the place is hot
13. b. Thursdays and Saturdays
14. c. around midnight
15. b. prancing
16. a. she makes their heart sing
17. b. yesterday
18. c. Who's your daddy?
19. c. good night
20. c. a pie in the face

****

HARDER QUESTIONS--Answers

1. c. a job
2. a. black
3. a. ashes
4. b. at a dance
5. a. walk along the shore

1. In *A World Without Love,* until Peter & Gordon can see their true love smile, what do they want you to do?

    a. laugh at them

    b. feel pity for them

    c. lock them away

****

2. While going to *Surf City,* what do Jan & Dean say they'll do if their car breaks down along the way?

    a. they'll hitch a ride

    b. they'll catch a cab

    c. they'll tow it all the way there

****

3. What did the Box Tops' girlfriend say to them in *The Letter*?

    a. to leave her alone

    b. that she couldn't live without them

    c. that she's coming home

****

4. In *Set Me Free,* if the Kinks can't have you to themselves, who do they have left?

    a. only themselves

    b. strangers with no names

    c. no one

****

5. In *You Only Live Twice,* Nancy Sinatra says that you live one life for yourself and one for _____.

    a. your lover

    b. your dreams

    c. other people's desires

6. What are *Lies* doing to the Knickerbockers?

    a. lies are making their love stronger
    b. lies are breaking their heart
    c. lies are getting them into more trouble

****

7. According to the Royal Guardsmen in *Snoopy's Christmas,* what did the Red Baron cry out to Snoopy after he made Snoopy land behind the enemy lines?

    a. Merry Christmas!
    b. So long, hound dog!
    c. We're even, my friend!

****

8. When the Monkees say to take the *Last Train to Clarksville,* where do they plan to meet you?

    a. on the train
    b. at their house
    c. at the station

****

9. In *God Only Knows,* what do the Beach Boys say would happen if you should ever leave them?

    a. life would still go on
    b. they'd go crazy
    c. they would vow never to marry

****

10. In *When the Lovelight Starts Shining Through His Eyes,* what did the Supremes realize that they should do?

    a. apologize
    b. run and hide
    c. forget the past and live for today

11. Where does the Beatles' *Long and Winding Road* lead to ?

        a. paradise

        b. your door

        c. a dead-end street

****

12. In *Who'll Stop the Rain,* what does Creedence Clearwater Revival say is on the ground ?

        a. confusion

        b. hungry hearts

        c. people drowning in their tears

****

13. According to Crosby, Stills & Nash, toward what famous city would you take the *Marrakesh Express* southbound to reach Marrakesh ?

        a. Tripoli

        b. Casablanca

        c. Woodstock

****

14. What problem is caused for B. J. Thomas as *Raindrops Keep Falling on My Head* ?

        a. he's drowning in love

        b. he can't stop the rain from falling

        c. nothing seems to fit

****

15. In *How Can I Be Sure,* what are the Young Rascals unsure about?

        a. whether you really love them

        b. whether they'll be sure with you

        c. whether there's school tomorrow

16. According to It's a Beautiful Day, where is the
    White Bird ?
    a. flying free in the deep blue sky
    b. in a golden cage
    c. in a mythical land looking for love

    ★★

17. In *Yester-Me, Yester-You, Yesterday,* how does
    Stevie Wonder feel when he recalls what he had ?
    a. he's happy for all the good times
    b. he wonders how he let it all slip away
    c. he feels lost and sad

    ★★

18. In *My Generation,* what do the Who ask the older
    generation to do ?
    a. fade away
    b. get with it
    c. dance to the beat

    ★★

19. What does Mary Hopkin fondly recall about *Those
    Were the Days* ?
    a. she thought they'd never end
    b. they were the best years of her life
    c. it's a miracle that she survived at all

    ★★

20. What do the Blades of Grass say that *Happy* is ?
    a. taking a walk on a sunny afternoon
    b. the day they found you
    c. when you're smiling

HARDER QUESTIONS: Worth 2 points each — 4 points if you can answer the question without the three choices!

****

1. What is Elvis Presley doing on the lonely back road in the *Kentucky Rain*?

   a. looking for you
   b. thumbing for a ride
   c. trying to find his way back home

****

2. In *Darlin'*, what does the love you give them do to the Beach Boys?

   a. it softens their life
   b. it keeps them satisfied
   c. it makes them more and more insecure

****

3. In *Do You Know the Way to San Jose*, what does Dionne Warwick say becomes of weeks in L.A.?

   a. they crawl by so slowly
   b. they seem like a dream
   c. they turn quickly into years

****

4. In *On the Way Home*, how can you tell Buffalo Springfield's dream is real?

   a. by the look in their eyes
   b. because they love you
   c. because home is where the heart is

****

5. What is Allan Sherman going to do with all the presents he has received during the *Twelve Days of Christmas*?

   a. donate them to charity
   b. open them up next year
   c. exchange them

ANSWERS

****

1. c. lock them away
2. a. they'll hitch a ride
3. b. that she couldn't live without them
4. c. no one
5. b. your dreams
6. b. lies are breaking their heart
7. a. Merry Christmas!
8. c. at the station
9. a. life would still go on
10. a. apologize
11. b. your door
12. a. confusion
13. b. Casablanca
14. c. nothing seems to fit
15. b. whether they'll be sure with you
16. b. in a golden cage
17. c. he feels lost and sad
18. a. fade away
19. a. she thought they'd never end
20. b. the day they found you

****

HARDER QUESTIONS--Answers

1. b. thumbing for a ride
2. a. it softens their life
3. c. they turn quickly into years
4. b. because they love you
5. c. exchange them

ROCK

TITLES

QUESTIONS

If you're brave enough to test your skills,
here's a simple SCORING CHART:

(questions are worth 1 point each — "Harder Questions"
are worth 2 points each . . . If you are able to correctly
answer the question/identify the song without the three
choices, you receive twice the point value!)

If you score . . .

25+ Points: You probably STILL think it's 1967!
(Check your wardrobe!)

20–24: You probably paid more attention to
rock & roll than books & school!
(Check your report card!)

15–19: There's a lot of rock & roll memories
in your blood!
*(But maybe it's time to buy
a few more rock & roll LPs!)*

10–14: Don't you wish you'd listened more closely
to rock & roll?!
(It's never too late to be hip!)

0–9: Where were YOU when rock began to rule?!
*(Time to get experienced —
run to your music store now!!!)*

(note: all answers are derived from lyrics within the song)

1. *The colors of the rainbow* are also on *the faces of people going by.*
   a. What a Wonderful World/Louis Armstrong
   b. England Swings/Roger Miller
   c. People/Barbra Streisand

****

2. *The people bowed and prayed to the neon god they made.*
   a. Sunshine Superman/Donovan
   b. The Sounds of Silence/Simon & Garfunkel
   c. Funky Broadway/Wilson Pickett

****

3. They're riding around the world . . . and trying to meet some girl, who tells them that they'd *better come back maybe next week* because she's *on a losing streak.*
   a. Can't Buy Me Love/Beatles
   b. (I Can't Get No) Satisfaction/Rolling Stones
   c. I Get Around/Beach Boys

****

4. *Sugar Pie Honey Bunch.*
   a. Apples, Peaches, Pumpkin Pie/Jay & the Techniques
   b. Sweet Soul Music/Arthur Conley
   c. I Can't Help Myself/Four Tops

****

5. *Inside this cold and empty house* they *dwell.*
   a. My World Is Empty Without You/Supremes
   b. You Were On My Mind/We Five
   c. Walk Away Renee/Left Banke

6. They want to *take a lover's vow and then seal it with a kiss.*
   - a. For Your Love/Yardbirds
   - b. The Look of Love/Sergio Mendes & Brasil '66
   - c. See You In September/Happenings

****

7. Yesterday his life *was filled with rain,* but then you smiled at him *and really eased the pain.*
   - a. Sunny/Bobby Hebb
   - b. Cherry Cherry/Neil Diamond
   - c. 98.6/Keith

****

8. *Doo-be-doo-be-doo-doo-doo-doo-dee-da.*
   - a. Shoo-Be-Doo-Be-Doo-Da-Day/Stevie Wonder
   - b. Um, Um, Um, Um, Um, Um/Major Lance
   - c. Strangers In the Night/Frank Sinatra

****

9. *If you're looking to find love you can share, all you've got to do is hold him and kiss him and love him and show him that you care.*
   - a. Baby, I'm Yours/Barbara Lewis
   - b. I Couldn't Live Without Your Love/Petula Clark
   - c. Wishin' and Hopin'/Dusty Springfield

****

10. They *don't claim to be an A student,* but they're trying to be one because maybe then they *can win your love for* them.
    - a. Wonderful World/Herman's Hermits
    - b. Carrie-Ann/Hollies
    - c. You Really Got Me/Kinks

11. *Those schoolgirl days of telling tales and biting nails are gone.*
   a. Come Back When You Grow Up/Bobby Vee
   b. To Sir With Love/Lulu
   c. These Boots Are Made for Walkin'/Nancy Sinatra

****

12. *Think of all the hate there is in Red China, then take a look around to Selma, Alabama.*
   a. Eve of Destruction/Barry McGuire
   b. Love Is All Around/Troggs
   c. The Times They Are A-Changin'/Peter, Paul & Mary

****

13. He *wants you for* his *sweet pet, but you keep playing hard to get.*
   a. Foxy Lady/Jimi Hendrix
   b. Dizzy/Tommy Roe
   c. Lightnin' Strikes/Lou Christie

****

14. *One fine day* he'll *find a way to move away from this old shack.*
   a. Poor Side of Town/Johnny Rivers
   b. Sugar Shack/Jimmy Gilmer & the Fireballs
   c. Down In the Boondocks/Billy Joe Royal

****

15. She wants you to do this *if you see* her *walking down the street and* she *starts to cry* each time you and she meet.
   a. You Don't Have to Say You Love Me/Dusty Springfield
   b. Rescue Me/Fontella Bass
   c. Walk on By/Dionne Warwick

16. When you're with them, *the skies will be blue* for all their life.
    a. Happy Together/Turtles
    b. Black Is Black/Los Bravos
    c. I Think We're Alone Now/Tommy James & the Shondells

****

17. *The pumps don't work 'cause the vandals took the handles.*
    a. Dirty Water/Standells
    b. Ain't That Peculiar/Marvin Gaye
    c. Subterranean Homesick Blues/Bob Dylan

****

18. *She's a pearl of a girl.*
    a. My Girl/Temptations
    b. Black Pearl/Sonny Charles
    c. Uptight (Everything's Alr ight)/Stevie Wonder

****

19. Since you've found her, everything she touches *is turning to gold.*
    a. How Does That Grab You Darlin'/Nancy Sinatra
    b. Color My World/Petula Clark
    c. Goldfinger/Shirley Bassey

****

20. *There was love all around, but they never heard it singing.*
    a. Willow Weep for Me/Chad & Jeremy
    b. Till There Was You/Beatles
    c. Bye, Bye Baby (Baby Goodbye)/Four Seasons

HARDER QUESTIONS: Worth 2 points each — 4 points if you can NAME THAT TUNE without the three choices !

****

1. *Caterpillar sheds his skin to find a butterfly within.*
   - a. There Is a Mountain/Donovan
   - b. A Beautiful Morning/Rascals
   - c. Elusive Butterfly/Bob Lind

****

2. *The windshield wipers seemed to say "together" and now they're saying "never".*
   - a. Can't You Hear My Heartbeat/Herman's Hermits
   - b. I'm So Lonesome I Could Cry/B. J. Thomas
   - c. Rhapsody In the Rain/Lou Christie

****

3. *The only one for* him *can only be you —* his *arms won't free you and* his *heart won't try.*
   - a. Green Green Grass of Home/Tom Jones
   - b. The More I See You/Chris Montez
   - c. A Place In the Sun/Stevie Wonder

****

4. *You treat* them *just like dirt — you have all the fun,* they *stay at home and hurt.*
   - a. I'm a Fool/Dino, Desi & Billy
   - b. Him Or Me—What's It Gonna Be/Paul Revere & the Raiders
   - c. Tired of Waiting for You/Kinks

****

5. You have stood by them *in their darkest hour.*
   - a. Oh Happy Day/Edwin Hawkins Singers
   - b. Oh How Happy/Shades of Blue
   - c. Wonderful! Wonderful!/Tymes

ANSWERS

****

1. a. What a Wonderful World/Louis Armstrong
2. b. The Sounds of Silence/Simon & Garfunkel
3. b. (I Can't Get No) Satisfaction/Rolling Stones
4. c. I Can't Help Myself/Four Tops
5. a. My World Is Empty Without You/Supremes
6. b. The Look of Love/Sergio Mendes & Brasil '66
7. a. Sunny/Bobby Hebb
8. c. Strangers In the Night/Frank Sinatra
9. c. Wishin' and Hopin '/Dusty Springfield
10. a. Wonderful World/Herman's Hermits
11. b. To Sir With Love/Lulu
12. a. Eve of Destruction/Barry McGuire
13. b. Dizzy/Tommy Roe
14. c. Down In the Boondocks/Billy Joe Royal
15. c. Walk on By/Dionne Warwick
16. a. Happy Together/Turtles
17. c. Subterranean Homesick Blues/Bob Dylan
18. c. Uptight (Everything's Alright)/Stevie Wonder
19. b. Color My World/Petula Clark
20. b. Till There Was You/Beatles

****

HARDER QUESTIONS--Answers

1. a. There Is a Mountain/Donovan
2. c. Rhapsody In the Rain/Lou Christie
3. b. The More I See You/Chris Montez
4. a. I'm a Fool/Dino, Desi & Billy
5. b. Oh How Happy/Shades of Blue

1. *By August,* she was theirs.
   - a. Bus Stop/Hollies
   - b. My Girl/Temptations
   - c. A Groovy Kind of Love/Mindbenders

****

2. *There's a man at* their *house, he's so big and strong—he goes to work each day and stays all day long.*
   - a. Father Sebastian/Ramblers
   - b. Co lor Him Father/Winstons
   - c. I'll Never Find Another You/Seekers

****

3. They'll *all be gone for the summer;* they're *on safari to stay.*
   - a. Surf City/Jan & Dean
   - b. Summer Means Fun/Rip Chords
   - c. Surfin' U.S.A./Beach Boys

****

4. *It really happened just this way* the day her mama socked it to them.
   - a. Harper Valley P.T.A./Jeannie C. Riley
   - b. Ode to Billie Joe/Bobbie Gentry
   - c. You Better Sit Down Kids/Cher

****

5. With *her long blonde hair,* she *made a ride that caused a scene in the town.*
   - a. Valleri/Monkees
   - b. Lady Godiva/Peter & Gordon
   - c. Jenny Take a Ride/Mitch Ryder & the Detroit Wheels

6. *They don't want to sound complaining but you know there's always rain in* their *heart.*
   - a. Please Please Me/Beatles
   - b. I'm Into Something Good/Herman's Hermits
   - c. Don't Let Me Be Misunderstood/Animals

****

7. *You're way on top since you left* them — *you're always laughing way down at* them.
   - a. Come a Little Bit Closer/Jay & the Americans
   - b. I Can't Let Go/Hollies
   - c. 96 Tears/? & the Mysterians

****

8. Their mama said that *love don't come easy — it's a game of give-and-take.*
   - a. A Little Bit Me, A Little Bit You/Monkees
   - b. You Can't Hurry Love/Supremes
   - c. The Rain, The Park & Other Things/Cowsills

****

9. They want you to *go away from* their *window* and *leave at your own chosen speed.*
   - a. It Ain't Me Babe/Turtles
   - b. Get Off of My Cloud/Rolling Stones
   - c. Time Won't Let Me/Outsiders

****

10. When he sees you *out and about, it's such a crime.*
    - a. Last Chance to Turn Around/Gene Pitney
    - b. Little Things/Bobby Goldsboro
    - c. It's Not Unusual/Tom Jones

11. They *have* their *books and* their *poetry to protect them.*

      a. I Am A Rock/Simon & Garfunkel
      b. When I Was Young/Animals
      c. Silence Is Golden/Tremeloes

****

12. They *didn't know if it was day or night.*

      a. A Hard Day's Night/Beatles
      b. Love Potion Number Nine/Searchers
      c. All Day & All of the Night/Kinks

****

13. *He didn't even say goodbye; he didn't take the time to write.*

      a. Love Is a Hurtin' Thing/Lou Rawls
      b. The Pied Piper/Crispian St. Peters
      c. Bang Bang (My Baby Shot Me Down)/Cher

****

14. *If you leave* them *a hundred times, a hundred times* they'll *take you back.*

      a. This Old Heart of Mine/Isley Brothers
      b. Reach Out I'll Be There/Four Tops
      c. Mercy, Mercy, Mercy/Buckinghams

****

15. They'll *pretend* they *are kissing the lips* they *are missing and hope that* their *dreams will come true.*

      a. Because/Dave Clark Five
      b. All My Lovin'/Beatles
      c. I'll Be There/Gerry & the Pacemakers

16. It *had two big horns and a wooly jaw.*

    a. Wooly Bully/Sam the Sham & the Pharaohs
    b. Beauty Is Only Skin Deep/Temptations
    c. The Hunter Gets Captured By the Game/Marvelettes

****

17. They want to you to do this *on the floor* because they want to dance with you.

    a. Let It Out (Let It All Hang Out)/Hombres
    b. Get On Up/Esquires
    c. Bend Me, Shape Me/American Breed

****

18. *Tuesday is so slow.*

    a. Brown-Eyed Girl/Van Morrison
    b. Tuesday Afternoon/Moody Blues
    c. Friday on My Mind/Easybeats

****

19. She says that you keep lying *when you ought to be truthin'* and you keep losing *when you ought to not bet.*

    a. Think/Aretha Franklin
    b. Anyone Who Had a Heart/Dionne Warwick
    c. These Boots Are Made for Walkin'/Nancy Sinatra

****

20. They *never gave a thought for tomorrow — just let tomorrow be.*

    a. I'm a Believer/Monkees
    b. Let's Live for Today/Grass Roots
    c. Summer Rain/Johnny Rivers

HARDER QUESTIONS: Worth 2 points each — 4 points if you can NAME THAT TUNE without the three choices !

****

1. *You tried to fool* them, *but* they *got wise — now* they won't listen to your dirty lies.
   - **a.** I See the Light/Five Americans
   - **b.** It's All Over Now/Rolling Stones
   - **c.** Pushin' Too Hard/Seeds

****

2. They'd *rather say "I do" than say "Goodbye".*
   - **a.** On a Carousel/Hollies
   - **b.** You Know What I Mean/Turtles
   - **c.** Hello Goodbye/Beatles

****

3. *They say that all good things must end someday — autumn leaves must fall — but don't you know* it hurts them so *to say goodbye to you.*
   - **a.** See You In September/Happenings
   - **b.** A World Without Love/Peter & Gordon
   - **c.** A Summer Song/Chad & Jeremy

****

4. She never walks alone and is *forever talking on the phone.*
   - **a.** Society's Child/Janis Ian
   - **b.** Talk Talk/Music Machine
   - **c.** Here Comes My Baby/Tremeloes

****

5. *Wedlock is nigh, my love.*
   - **a.** Green Grass/Gary Lewis & the Playboys
   - **b.** Winchester Cathedral/New Vaudeville Band
   - **c.** Lady Jane/Rolling Stones

ANSWERS

****

1. a. Bus Stop/Hollies
2. b. Color Him Father/Winstons
3. c. Surfin' U.S.A./Beach Boys
4. a. Harper Valley P.T.A./Jeannie C. Riley
5. b. Lady Godiva/Peter & Gordon
6. a. Please Please Me/Beatles
7. c. 96 Tears/? (Question Mark) & the Mysterians
8. b. You Can't Hurry Love/Supremes
9. a. It Ain't Me Babe/Turtles
10. c. It's Not Unusual/Tom Jones
11. a. I Am A Rock/Simon & Garfunkel
12. b. Love Potion Number Nine/Searchers
13. c. Bang Bang (My Baby Shot Me Down)/Cher
14. a. This Old Heart of Mine/Isley Brothers
15. b. All My Lovin'/Beatles
16. a. Wooly Bully/Sam the Sham & the Pharaohs
17. b. Get On Up/Esquires
18. a. Brown-Eyed Girl/Van Morrison
19. c. These Boots Are Made for Walkin'/Nancy Sinatra
20. c. Summer Rain/Johnny Rivers

****

HARDER QUESTIONS--Answers

1. a. I See the Light/Five Americans
2. b. You Know What I Mean/Turtles
3. c. A Summer Song/Chad & Jeremy
4. c. Here Comes My Baby/Tremeloes
5. c. Lady Jane/Rolling Stones

1. *You've got to learn how to Pony like Bony Maroney.*
    a. Shake/Sam Cooke
    b. Barefootin'/Robert Parker
    c. Land of 1,000 Dances/Wilson Pickett

****

2. He has *only one burning desire.*
    a. Laugh At Me/Sonny
    b. Fire/Jimi Hendrix
    c. Positively 4th Street/Bob Dylan

****

3. *When you move up close to* them, they *get a feeling that's oooweeee.*
    a. Can't You Hear My Heartbeat/Herman's Hermits
    b. Do You Believe In Magic/Lovin' Spoonful
    c. A Groovy Kind of Love/Mindbenders

****

4. They're *smoking cigarettes and watching Captain Kangaroo.*
    a. Turn-Down Day/Cyrkle
    b. Lazy Day/Spanky & Our Gang
    c. Flowers on the Wall/Statler Brothers

****

5. They'll *do funny things if you want* them *to.*
    a. Laugh, Laugh/Beau Brummels
    b. I'm Your Puppet/James & Bobby Purify
    c. Oh How Happy/Shades of Blue

6. They would yell this *with all of* their *might*.
   - a. Catch Us If You Can/Dave Clark Five
   - b. Help!/Beatles
   - c. I'm a Man/Spencer Davis Group

****

7. Follow him and he'll *show you where it's at*.
   - a. Seventh Son/Johnny Rivers
   - b. The Pied Piper/Crispian St. Peters
   - c. C'mon and Swim/Bobby Freeman

****

8. *You might like to hear on* their *organ "Ride Sally Ride"*.
   - a. Dance to the Music/Sly & the Family Stone
   - b. In the Midnight Hour/Young Rascals
   - c. Keep On Dancing/Gentrys

****

9. As soon as love came into their heart, *you turned and walked away*.
   - a. Love Is Here And Now You're Gone/Supremes
   - b. Sure Gonna Miss Her/Gary Lewis & the Playboys
   - c. (I Know) I'm Losing You/Temptations

****

10. *Please remember me to the one who lives there — she once was a true love of mine.*
    - a. Everlasting Love/Robert Knight
    - b. Scarborough Fair/Simon & Garfunkel
    - c. A Whiter Shade of Pale/Procol Harum

11. *Drums keep pounding a rhythm to the brain.*
   a. Pata Pata/Miriam Makeba
   b. Cold Sweat/James Brown
   c. The Beat Goes On/Sonny & Cher

****

12. *Hello lamp post, whatcha knowin'* — they *come to watch your flowers growin'.*
   a. Leaning on the Lamp Post/Herman's Hermits
   b. The 59th Street Bridge Song (Feelin' Groovy)/Harpers Bizarre
   c. I'd Like to Get to Know You/Spanky & Our Gang

****

13. He *needed the shelter of someone's arms, and there you were.*
   a. How Sweet It Is To Be Loved By You/Marvin Gaye
   b. Higher and Higher/Jackie Wilson
   c. Honey/Bobby Goldsboro

****

14. They saw a film today in which the English *had just won the war.*
   a. Summertime Blues/Blue Cheer
   b. Jumpin' Jack Flash/Rolling Stones
   c. A Day In the Life/Beatles

****

15. *Every time he says he loves* them, *chills run down* their *spine.*
   a. The Boy From New York City/Ad Libs
   b. Baby Love/Supremes
   c. Heat Wave/Martha & the Vandellas

16. *In the chilly hours and minutes of uncertainty,* he wants to be *in the warm hold of your loving mind.*
    - a. Catch the Wind/Donovan
    - b. The More I See You/Chris Montez
    - c. Sweet Pea/Tommy Roe

****

17. *If you're not going to stay, please don't tease* her *like you did before* because she still loves you so.
    - a. Don't Sleep In the Subway/Petula Clark
    - b. Hello Stranger/Barbara Lewis
    - c. I Only Want to Be With You/Dusty Springfield

****

18. He'd *turn his back on his best friend* if the friend put her down.
    - a. Tell It Like It Is/Aaron Neville
    - b. You Turn Me On/Ian Whitcomb
    - c. When a Man Loves a Woman/Percy Sledge

****

19. *No longer can* they *walk these paths for they have changed —* they *must be on, the sun is gone, and* they *think it's gonna rain.*
    - a. Hazy Shade of Winter/Simon & Garfunkel
    - b. Sunday Will Never Be the Same/Spanky & Our Gang
    - c. Stormy/Classics IV

****

20. *No one's getting fat except* her.
    - a. Bernadette/Four Tops
    - b. A Must to Avoid/Herman's Hermits
    - c. Creeque Alley/the Mamas & the Papas

HARDER QUESTIONS: Worth 2 points each — 4 points if you can NAME THAT TUNE without the three choices !

****

1. *He rode an old gray mare called Bess, searching for a damsel in distress.*
   - a. Conquistador/Procol Harum
   - b. Knight In Rusty Armour/Peter & Gordon
   - c. Gitarzan/Ray Stevens

****

2. *Then came the dawn, and you were gone — you were gone, gone, gone.*
   - a. Black Is Black/Los Bravos
   - b. I Saw Her Again/The Mamas & the Papas
   - c. I Had Too Much To Dream Last Night/Electric Prunes

****

3. *Ring those bells.*
   - a. Ding Dong the Witch Is Dead/Fifth Estate
   - b. Summertime/Billy Stewart
   - c. Sweet Blindness/5ᵗʰ Dimension

****

4. *Cast your tears into the sea — don't waste those good tears on* them.
   - a. Don't Throw Your Love Away/Searchers
   - b. Not the Lovin' Kind/Dino, Desi & Billy
   - c. Shades of Grey/Monkees

****

5. *You give them a feeling in* their *heart like an arrow passing through it.*
   - a. Nobody I Know/Peter & Gordon
   - b. The Way You Do the Things You Do/Temptations
   - c. How Do You Do It/Gerry & the Pacemakers

ANSWERS

****

1. c. Land of 1,000 Dances/Wilson Pickett
2. b. Fire/Jimi Hendrix
3. a. Can't You Hear My Heartbeat/Herman's Hermits
4. c. Flowers on the Wall/Statler Brothers
5. b. I'm Your Puppet/James & Bobby Purify
6. a. Catch Us If You Can/Dave Clark Five
7. b. The Pied Piper/Crispian St. Peters
8. a. Dance to the Music/Sly & the Family Stone
9. a. Love Is Here And Now You're Gone/Supremes
10. b. Scarborough Fair/Simon & Garfunkel
11. c. The Beat Goes On/Sonny & Cher
12. b. The 59th Street Bridge Song (Feelin' Groovy)/Harpers
13. a. How Sweet It Is To Be Loved By You/Marvin Gaye
14. c. A Day In the Life/Beatles
15. a. The Boy From New York City/Ad Libs
16. a. Catch the Wind/Donovan
17. b. Hello Stranger/Barbara Lewis
18. c. When a Man Loves a Woman/Percy Sledge
19. b. Sunday Will Never Be the Same/Spanky & Our Gang
20. c. Creeque Alley/the Mamas & the Papas

****

HARDER QUESTIONS--Answers

1. b. Knight In Rusty Armour/Peter & Gordon
2. c. I Had Too Much To Dream Last Night/Electric Prunes
3. a. Ding Dong the Witch Is Dead/Fifth Estate
4. b. Not the Lovin' Kind/Dino, Desi & Billy
5. c. How Do You Do It/Gerry & the Pacemakers

1. When they get up in the morning, they're *filled with desire* because love is *a real live wire.*
    a. You're the One/Vogues
    b. Love Is Like an Itching In My Heart/Supremes
    c. You Were On My Mind/We Five

****

2. She's *a big teaser — she took* them *half the way there.*
    a. Day Tripper/Beatles
    b. Come Home/Dave Clark Five
    c. Tired of Waiting for You/Kinks

****

3. *What a drag it is getting old.*
    a. We Gotta Get Out of This Place/Animals
    b. Mother's Little Helper/Rolling Stones
    c. My Generation/Who

****

4. It seems to them that *we've got to solve our problems individually.*
    a. You've Got Your Troubles/Fortunes
    b. Sweet Cherry Wine/Tommy James & the Shondells
    c. People Got to Be Free/Rascals

****

5. He's gonna save all his money, *get a helmet and roll-bar* and he'll be ready to go — *little buddy, gonna shut you down.*
    a. Shut Down/Beach Boys
    b. Three Window Coupe/Rip Chords
    c. G.T.O./Ronny & the Daytonas

6. She *lives in a very bad part of town.*
   - a. Sugar Town/Nancy Sinatra
   - b. Hang On Sloopy/McCoys
   - c. Rag Doll/Four Seasons

****

7. *Perish is the word that more than applies to the hope in* their *heart each time* they *realize that* they *are not going to be the one to share your dreams.*
   - a. Cherish/Association
   - b. Standing In the Shadows of Love/Four Tops
   - c. To Love Somebody/Bee Gees

****

8. They *feel like* they *can't go on without love.*
   - a. (I've Been) Lonely Too Long/Young Rascals
   - b. I Don't Want to Spoil the Party/Beatles
   - c. Nothing But Heartaches/Supremes

****

9. They tell themselves that they *didn't lose her, because you can't lose a friend you never had.*
   - a. Kind of a Drag/Buckinghams
   - b. I Can See For Miles/Who
   - c. I Wonder What She's Doing Tonight/Tommy Boyce & Bobby Hart

****

10. They're *not content to be with you in the daytime.*
   - a. Let's Spend the Night Together/Rolling Stones
   - b. All Day & All of the Night/Kinks
   - c. Good Thing/Paul Revere & the Raiders

11. They *never saw the good side of a city until* they *hitched a ride on the riverboat queen.*
   a. Come on Down to My Boat/Every Mother's Son
   b. Proud Mary/Creedence Clearwater Revival
   c. Born to Be Wild/Steppenwolf
****

12. They're *not in the market for a boy who wants to love only* them.
   a. You Can't Hurry Love/Supremes
   b. The End of Our Road/Gladys Knight & the Pips
   c. Different Drum/Stone Poneys
****

13. She's *gonna be a lady some day.*
   a. Baby Don't Go/Sonny & Cher
   b. Born a Woman/Sandy Posey
   c. Respect/Aretha Franklin
****

14. This is how he feels although *the wheat fields and the clothes lines and the junkyards and the highways come between* you and him.
   a. Gentle on My Mind/Glen Campbell
   b. Born Free/Matt Monro
   c. Uptight (Everything's Alright)/Stevie Wonder
****

15. *You know what they say about the bird in the hand, and that's why* they *ain't leaving without you.*
   a. Then You Can Tell Me Goodbye/Casinos
   b. La-La Means I Love You/Delfonics
   c. Sit Down I Think I Love You/Mojo Men

16. Though you're never near, *your voice* he *often hears.*

      a. Baby, I Need Your Lovin'/Johnny Rivers
      b. Girl, You'll Be a Woman Soon/Neil Diamond
      c. Crying In the Chapel/Elvis Presley

****

17. *The only sound that you will hear is when* they *whisper in your ear, "I love you".*

      a. I Love You/People
      b. Hello, I Love You/Doors
      c. There's a Kind of Hush/Herman's Hermits

****

18. *Now* their *life has changed in oh so many ways —* their *independence seems to have vanished in the haze.*

      a. I Wanna Be Free/Monkees
      b. Help!/Beatles
      c. Time Won't Let Me/Outsiders

****

19. *All across the nation,* there's *such a strange vibration* of *people in motion.*

      a. Summer In the City/Lovin' Spoonful
      b. Good Vibrations/Beach Boys
      c. San Francisco (Be Sure to Wear Some Flowers In Your Hair)/Scott McKenzie

****

20. Do this *if you feel that you can't go on because all of your hope is gone.*

      a. Reach Out I'll Be There/Four Tops
      b. Hold Me, Thrill Me, Kiss Me/Mel Carter
      c. Go Now/Moody Blues

HARDER QUESTIONS: Worth 2 points each — 4 points if you can NAME THAT TUNE without the three choices !

****

1. *You can't face the world with your head to the ground.*
   - a. Hush/Deep Purple
   - b. (We Ain't Got) Nothin' Yet/Blues Magoos
   - c. Georgy Girl/Seekers

****

2. As long as you don't do this, you can *go out and have your fun . . . with anyone.*
   - a. Don't Let Me Be Misunderstood/Animals
   - b. Don't Sleep In the Subway/Petula Clark
   - c. Don't Throw Your Love Away/Searchers

****

3. They *told him* they *were going to be a star, but to do it* they *would have to go far away.*
   - a. Western Union/Five Americans
   - b. Next Plane to London/Rose Garden
   - c. Just Dropped In/First Edition

****

4. *Seasons change with the scenery, weaving time in a tapestry.*
   - a. A Hazy Shade of Winter/Simon & Garfunkel
   - b. Blowin' In the Wind/Peter, Paul & Mary
   - c. Cowboys to Girls/Intruders

****

5. They want him to *play a tune to make* them *happy.*
   - a. Happy Jack/Who
   - b. Mr. Tambourine Man/Byrds
   - c. Dear Mr. Fantasy/Traffic

ANSWERS

****

1. b. Love Is Like an Itching In My Heart/Supremes
2. a. Day Tripper/Beatles
3. b. Mother's Little Helper/Rolling Stones
4. c. People Got to Be Free/Rascals
5. c. G.T.O./Ronny & the Daytonas
6. b. Hang On Sloopy/McCoys
7. a. Cherish/Association
8. a. (I've Been) Lonely Too Long/Young Rascals
9. c. I Wonder What She's Doing Tonight/Tommy Boyce & Bobby Hart
10. b. All Day & All of the Night/Kinks
11. b. Proud Mary/Creedence Clearwater Revival
12. c. Different Drum/Stone Poneys
13. a. Baby Don't Go/Sonny & Cher
14. a. Gentle on My Mind/Glen Campbell
15. c. Sit Down I Think I Love You/Mojo Men
16. a. Baby, I Need Your Lovin'/Johnny Rivers
17. c. There's a Kind of Hush/Herman's Hermits
18. b. Help!/Beatles
19. c. San Francisco/Scott McKenzie
20. a. Reach Out I'll Be There/Four Tops

****

HARDER QUESTIONS--Answers

1. b. (We Ain't Got) Nothin' Yet/Blues Magoos
2. c. Don't Throw Your Love Away/Searchers
3. b. Next Plane to London/Rose Garden
4. a. A Hazy Shade of Winter/Simon & Garfunkel
5. c. Dear Mr. Fantasy/Traffic

1. *Nobody's right if everybody's wrong.*
   - a. We Can Work It Out/Beatles
   - b. Psychotic Reaction/Count Five
   - c. For What It's Worth/Buffalo Springfield

****

2. *She's gonna get a ticket sooner or later because she can't keep her foot off the accelerator.*
   - a. Fun, Fun, Fun/Beach Boys
   - b. The Little Old Lady From Pasadena/Jan & Dean
   - c. G.T.O./Ronny & the Daytonas

****

3. If you really love them, tell them they are through, because *no words of consolation will make* them *miss you less.*
   - a. Susan/Buckinghams
   - b. Reflections/Supremes
   - c. Make It Easy on Yourself/Walker Brothers

****

4. They *still remember when you used to be nine years old.*
   - a. Together/Intruders
   - b. Shout/Isley Brothers
   - c. Traces/Classics IV

****

5. *You thought* they'd *need a crystal ball to see right through the haze.*
   - a. I Can See For Miles/Who
   - b. Crystal Blue Persuasion/Tommy James & the Shondells
   - c. Judy In Disguise (With Glasses)/John Fred & His Playboy Band

6. *There she was just walking down the street —*
   snapping her fingers and shuffling her feet.
   - a. Do Wah Diddy Diddy/Manfred Mann
   - b. Ob-La-Di, Ob-La-Da/Beatles
   - c. Skinny Legs and All/Joe Tex

****

7. If they were given a fortune, their pleasure *would*
   be small — they *could lose it all tomorrow and*
   never mind at all.
   - a. I'll Never Find Another You/Seekers
   - b. All I Need/Temptations
   - c. Nashville Cats/Lovin' Spoonful

****

8. *You say you fear* that they'll change their mind and
   that they *won't require you.*
   - a. Never My Love/Association
   - b. Dedicated to the One I Love/The Mamas & the Papas
   - c. I Can't Help Myself/Four Tops

****

9. They want to know *whatever happened to all the*
   good times they *used to have — the times* they
   cried and laughed.
   - a. Pretty Ballerina/Left Banke
   - b. As Tears Go By/Rolling Stones
   - c. Don't You Care/Buckinghams

****

10. *It's wrong to say* they *don't think of you, 'cause*
    when you say these things, it makes them *blue.*
    - a. Because/Dave Clark Five
    - b. God Only Knows/Beach Boys
    - c. Just Once In My Life/Righteous Brothers

11. *Sometimes* they *find* themselves *alone and regretting some foolish thing, some little thing* they've *done.*
   a. I Go To Pieces/Peter & Gordon
   b. No Milk Today/Herman's Hermits
   c. Don't Let Me Be Misunderstood/Animals

****

12. *Today said the time was right* for them *to follow you.*
   a. Younger Girl/Critters
   b. You Didn't Have to Be So Nice/Lovin' Spoonful
   c. Daydream Believer/Monkees

****

13. Their *heart went boom when* they *crossed that room* and they held her hand in theirs.
   a. I Saw Her Standing There/Beatles
   b. I Like It/Gerry & the Pacemakers
   c. Angelito/Rene & Rene

****

14. *Do the Watusi like* their *girl Lucy.*
   a. Land of 1,000 Dances/Cannibal & the Headhunters
   b. Keep On Dancing/Gentrys
   c. Sock It To Me Baby/Mitch Ryder & the Detroit Wheels

****

15. She's been his inspiration, and *through thick and thin, our love just won't end.*
   a. Please Love Me Forever/Bobby Vinton
   b. I Was Made to Love Her/Stevie Wonder
   c. Dizzy/Tommy Roe

16. *He's oh so good, and he's oh so fine — and he's oh so healthy in his body and his mind.*
    a. Universal Soldier/Donovan
    b. The Ballad of the Green Berets/SSgt. Barry Sadler
    c. A Well Respected Man/Kinks

****

17. *They would give the stars above* to make you dream of them at night.
    a. Midnight Confessions/Grass Roots
    b. For Your Love/Yardbirds
    c. I Say Love/Royal Guardsmen

****

18. *Now* their *empty cup is as sweet as the punch.*
    a. Along Comes Mary/Association
    b. Summer Wine/Nancy Sinatra & Lee Hazlewood
    c. Double Shot/Swingin' Medallions

****

19. She's *always window-shopping but never stopping to buy.*
    a. Honey Chile/Martha & the Vandellas
    b. Georgy Girl/Seekers
    c. I Wonder What She's Doing Tonight/Tommy Boyce & Bobby Hart

****

20. *Walk along the lake with someone new, have yourself a summer fling or two, but remember* that they're *in love with you.*
    a. Save Your Heart for Me/Gary Lewis & the Playboys
    b. A Summer Song/Chad & Jeremy
    c. Andrea/Sunrays

HARDER QUESTIONS: Worth 2 points each — 4 points if you can NAME THAT TUNE without the three choices !

****

1. *The T.V.'s on the blink, made Galileo look like a Boy Scout.*

   a. A Little Bit O' Soul/Music Explosion
   b. Let It Out (Let It All Hang Out)/Hombres
   c. The Duck/Jackie Lee

****

2. *You can turn off and on more times than a flashing neon sign.*

   a. See See Rider/Animals
   b. Mustang Sally/Wilson Pickett
   c. Take It Or Leave It/Rolling Stones

****

3. *You've got to reap what you sow.*

   a. Turn! Turn! Turn!/Byrds
   b. It's Alright/J. J. Jackson
   c. Laugh Laugh/Beau Brummels

****

4. Even in their dreams they *look into your eyes;* suddenly it seems they've *found* their *paradise.*

   a. Just a Little Bit Better/Herman's Hermits
   b. I'm Telling You Now/Freddie & the Dreamers
   c. Nobody I Know/Peter & Gordon

****

5. *There ain't nothing it can't fix — old dogs can learn new tricks.*

   a. Walkin' My Cat Named Dog/Norma Tanega
   b. Acapulco Gold/Rainy Daze
   c. Rice Is Nice/Lemon Pipers

ANSWERS

****

1. c. For What It's Worth/Buffalo Springfield
2. b. The Little Old Lady From Pasadena/Jan & Dean
3. c. Make It Easy on Yourself/Walker Brothers
4. b. Shout/Isley Brothers
5. a. I Can See For Miles/Who
6. a. Do Wah Diddy Diddy/Manfred Mann
7. a. I'll Never Find Another You/Seekers
8. a. Never My Love/Association
9. c. Don't You Care/Buckinghams
10. a. Because/Dave Clark Five
11. c. Don't Let Me Be Misunderstood/Animals
12. b. You Didn't Have to Be So Nice/Lovin' Spoonful
13. a. I Saw Her Standing There/Beatles
14. a. Land of 1,000 Dances/Cannibal & the Headhunters
15. b. I Was Made to Love Her/Stevie Wonder
16. c. A Well Respected Man/Kinks
17. b. For Your Love/Yardbirds
18. a. Along Comes Mary/Association
19. b. Georgy Girl/Seekers
20. a. Save Your Heart for Me/Gary Lewis & the Playboys

****

HARDER QUESTIONS--Answers

1. b. Let It Out (Let It All Hang Out)/Hombres
2. c. Take It Or Leave It/Rolling Stones
3. b. It's Alright/J. J. Jackson
4. c. Nobody I Know/Peter & Gordon
5. b. Acapulco Gold/Rainy Daze

1. *You never close your eyes anymore when* they *kiss your lips.*
   a. You've Lost That Lovin' Feeling/Righteous Brothers
   b. Cry Like a Baby/Box Tops
   c. Come On React/Fireballs
   ****

2. Now for them things are *dreary,* and it's *windy and cold —* and they *stand alone in the rain calling your name.*
   a. 96 Tears/? & the Mysterians
   b. Windy/Association
   c. Stormy/Classics IV
   ****

3. Last night they *met a new girl in the neighborhood.*
   a. Do You Want to Know a Secret/Beatles
   b. I'm Into Something Good/Herman's Hermits
   c. New Girl In School/Jan & Dean
   ****

4. They're *gonna blow for you.*
   a. The Horse/Cliff Nobles & Company
   b. What Does It Take (To Win Your Love For Me)/
      Junior Walker & The All-Stars
   c. Tighten Up/Archie Bell & the Drells
   ****

5. He's *watching the ships roll in* and then he watches them *roll away again.*
   a. (Sittin' On) The Dock of the Bay/Otis Redding
   b. Twenty Five Miles/Edwin Starr
   c. Atlantis/Donovan

6. *Jesus loves you more than you will know.*
   a. Son of a Preacher Man/Dusty Springfield
   b. Everyday People/Sly & the Family Stone
   c. Mrs. Robinson/Simon & Garfunkel

****

7. *Now* they *need you more than ever — no excuses offered anyway.*
   a. Let's Spend the Night Together/Rolling Stones
   b. Love Is All Around/Troggs
   c. Time of the Season/Zombies

****

8. *Your touch has grown cold.*
   a. Crying Time/Ray Charles
   b. Yesterday's Gone/Chad & Jeremy
   c. (I Know) I'm Losing You/Temptations

****

9. *Baby,* they *can't make it without you.*
   a. Soul and Inspiration/Righteous Brothers
   b. Standing In the Shadows of Love/Four Tops
   c. Where Were You When I Needed You/Grass Roots

****

10. *Don't say you can't get any boy at all — don't be so smug* or else you'll find *you can't get any boy at all* . . . you'll wind up as a *lady sitting on the shelf.*
    a. Him Or Me—What's It Gonna Be/Paul Revere & the Raiders
    b. Tell It Like It Is/Aaron Neville
    c. Laugh, Laugh/Beau Brummels

11. They *miss kissing you,* so *don't throw* their *love away.*

     a. Don't Throw Your Love Away/Searchers

     b. Baby Love/Supremes

     c. Love Me Two Times/Doors

****

12. She *shines with her own kind of light.*

     a. Kentucky Woman/Neil Diamond

     b. Gloria/Them

     c. Sunny/Bobby Hebb

****

13. *Don't go out tonight* because *it's bound to take your life.*

     a. The Unicorn/Irish Rovers

     b. Bad Moon Rising/Creedence Clearwater Revival

     c. The River Is Wide/Grass Roots

****

14. Their *own beliefs are in* their *song.*

     a. Everyday People/Sly & the Family Stone

     b. Expressway to Your Heart/Soul Survivors

     c. Beauty Is Only Skin Deep/Temptations

****

15. *It's like thunder, lightning* — the way you love him *is frightening.*

     a. Lightnin' Strikes/Lou Christie

     b. Release Me/Engelbert Humperdinck

     c. Knock on Wood/Eddie Floyd

16. *The tax man's taken all* their *dough and left them in their stately home.*
   a. Sunny Afternoon/Kinks
   b. Taxman/Beatles
   c. We Gotta Get Out of This Place/Animals

****

17. She's *everything that a big bad wolf could want.*
   a. My Girl/Temptations
   b. Cara Mia/Jay & the Americans
   c. Li'l Red Riding Hood/Sam the Sham and the Pharaohs

****

18. *He asked the Great Pumpkin for a new battle plan.*
   a. Mr. Spaceman/Byrds
   b. Here Comes the Judge/Shorty Long
   c. Snoopy Versus the Red Baron/Royal Guardsmen

****

19. *She's been married seven times before.*
   a. Seventh Son/Johnny Rivers
   b. Ruby Tuesday/Rolling Stones
   c. I'm Henry VIII, I Am/Herman's Hermits

****

20. Yesterday *it rained in Tennessee,* and she heard that *it also rained in Tallahassee,* but *not a drop fell on little old me.*
   a. A Sign of the Times/Petula Clark
   b. I Say a Little Prayer/Dionne Warwick
   c. Sugartown/Nancy Sinatra

HARDER QUESTIONS: Worth 2 points each — 4 points if you can NAME THAT TUNE without the three choices !

****

1. *She said she'd never hurt* them *but then she turned around and broke* their *heart.*

>   a. Bad to Me/Billy J. Kramer & the Dakotas
>   b. She/Monkees
>   c. She's About a Mover/Sir Douglas Quintet

****

2. Because *the revolution's near . . . we have got to get it together now.*

>   a. I Can See For Miles/Who
>   b. Something In the Air/Thunderclap Newman
>   c. Revolution/Beatles

****

3. He *could have tripped out easy,* but he's changed his ways.

>   a. Yeh Yeh/Georgie Fame
>   b. Something's Gotten Hold Of My Heart/Gene Pitney
>   c. Sunshine Superman/Donovan

****

4. *She said she'd never been in trouble, not even in town.*

>   a. A Single Girl/Sandy Posey
>   b. Younger Girl/Lovin' Spoonful
>   c. Cinnamon/Derek

****

5. *If I don't meet you no more in this world, then I'll meet you in the next one.*

>   a. Voodoo Child/Jimi Hendrix
>   b. Break On Through to the Other Side/Doors
>   c. White Room/Cream

ANSWERS

****

1. a. You've Lost That Lovin' Feeling/Righteous Brothers
2. c. Stormy/Classics IV
3. b. I'm Into Something Good/Herman's Hermits
4. b. What Does It Take (To Win Your Love For Me)/Junior Walker & The All-Stars
5. a. (Sittin' On) The Dock of the Bay/Otis Redding
6. c. Mrs. Robinson/Simon & Garfunkel
7. a. Let's Spend the Night Together/Rolling Stones
8. c. (I Know) I'm Losing You/Temptations
9. a. Soul and Inspiration/Righteous Brothers
10. c. Laugh, Laugh/Beau Brummels
11. b. Baby Love/Supremes
12. a. Kentucky Woman/Neil Diamond
13. b. Bad Moon Rising/Creedence Clearwater Revival
14. a. Everyday People/Sly & the Family Stone
15. c. Knock on Wood/Eddie Floyd
16. a. Sunny Afternoon/Kinks
17. c. Li'l Red Riding Hood/Sam the Sham and the Pharaohs
18. c. Snoopy Versus the Red Baron/Royal Guardsmen
19. c. I'm Henry VIII, I Am/Herman's Hermits
20. c. Sugartown/Nancy Sinatra

****

HARDER QUESTIONS--Answers

1. b. She/Monkees
2. b. Something In the Air/Thunderclap Newman
3. c. Sunshine Superman/Donovan
4. b. Younger Girl/Lovin' Spoonful
5. a. Voodoo Child/Jimi Hendrix

1. She *didn't even know you — you couldn't have been too much more than ten.*
    a. Think/Aretha Franklin
    b. Son of a Preacher Man/Dusty Springfield
    c. Jackson/Nancy Sinatra
****

2. *Other girls may try to take* them *away, but it's by your side* they'll *stay.*
    a. Cara Mia/Jay & the Americans
    b. Glad All Over/Dave Clark Five
    c. Heart Full of Soul/Yardbirds
****

3. They don't need any *money, fortune or fame,* because they've *got all the riches one man can claim.*
    a. Can't Buy Me Love/Beatles
    b. Never My Love/Association
    c. My Girl/Temptations
****

4. *If you are serious, don't play with* his *heart — it* makes *him furious.*
    a. Tell It Like It Is/Aaron Neville
    b. Hold What You've Got/Joe Tex
    c. I'll Be Doggone/Marvin Gaye
****

5. *Look at the way* they've *got to hide what* they're *doing.*
    a. Game of Love/Wayne Fontana & the Mindbenders
    b. Love Child/Diana Ross & the Supremes
    c. I Think We're Alone Now/Tommy James & the Shondells

6. Their *smile is* their *makeup* they *wear since* their *breakup with you.*
   a. The Tracks of My Tears/Smokey Robinson & the Miracles
   b. Worst That Could Happen/Brooklyn Bridge
   c. Hurt So Bad/Lettermen

****

7. *The world cannot be wrong if in this world there is you.*
   a. This Is My Song/Petula Clark
   b. To Sir With Love/Lulu
   c. Can't Take My Eyes Off You/Frankie Valli

****

8. *You twinkle above us, you twinkle below.*
   a. Good Morning Starshine/Oliver
   b. Sunshine Superman/Donovan
   c. Sunshine of Your Love/Cream

****

9. Each time they tell themselves that they've had enough, they want to show you *that a woman can be tough.*
   a. Go Where You Wanna Go/5th Dimension
   b. You're All I Need to Get By/Marvin Gaye & Tammi Terrell
   c. Piece of My Heart/Big Brother & the Holding Company

****

10. *How can you tell* him *how much you've missed* him *when the last time* he *saw you, you wouldn't even kiss* him.
   a. Poor Side of Town/Johnny Rivers
   b. I Knew You When/Billy Joe Royal
   c. Like a Rolling Stone/Bob Dylan

11. *Reach out to* them *for satisfaction* and call their name *for quick reaction.*
    a. Reach Out of the Darkness/Friend & Lover
    b. Hold On I'm Comin'/Sam & Dave
    c. Reach Out I'll Be There/Four Tops

****

12. *Now the time has come* and so they *must go* even though they may *lose a friend in the end.*
    a. Willow Weep for Me/Chad & Jeremy
    b. Just a Little/Beau Brummels
    c. I'll Follow the Sun/Beatles

****

13. There'll be *red and yellow honey, sassafras and moonshine.*
    a. Stoned Soul Picnic/5th Dimension
    b. Grazin' In the Grass/Friends of Distinction
    c. Hot Fun In the Summertime/Sly & the Family Stone

****

14. She's *got your picture hanging on the wall.*
    a. Chain of Fools/Aretha Franklin
    b. I Couldn't Live Without Your Love/Petula Clark
    c. Ain't Nothing Like the Real Thing/Marvin Gaye & Tammi Terrell

****

15. If the *mountains should crumble to the sea,* he won't cry — he *won't shed a tear.*
    a. Love Is a Hurtin' Thing/Lou Rawls
    b. Stand By Me/Ben E. King
    c. Never Give You Up/Jerry Butler

16. They're *lost in a world made for you and* them.
    a. I Hear a Symphony/Supremes
    b. A World of Our Own/Seekers
    c. True Love Ways/Peter & Gordon

****

17. *All* she wants to do *is ride around.*
    a. Hurrah for Hazel/Tommy Roe
    b. Mustang Sally/Wilson Pickett
    c. Fun, Fun, Fun/Beach Boys

****

18. *It's written on the wind, it's everywhere* they *go.*
    a. Blowin' In the Wind/Peter, Paul & Mary
    b. Fever/McCoys
    c. Love Is All Around/Troggs

****

19. He feels nice, *like sugar and spice.*
    a. You Turn Me On/Ian Whitcomb
    b. I Got You (I Feel Good)/James Brown
    c. King of the Road/Roger Miller

****

20. *This world's gotta lot of space*, and if people
    don't like his *face,* it's not he who's planning to
    do anything different or go anywhere else —
    because *it's gotta start some place, it's gotta
    start sometime,* and maybe *the next guy that
    don't wear a silk tie can walk by and say "hi"
    instead of "why?".*
    a. See The Funny Little Clown/Bobby Goldsboro
    b. It's Not Unusual/Tom Jones
    c. Laugh At Me/Sonny Bono

HARDER QUESTIONS: Worth 2 points each — 4 points if you can NAME THAT TUNE without the three choices !

****

1. Now they *see life for what it is — it's not all dreams, it's not all bliss.*

   a. The Happening/Supremes
   b. This Door Swings Both Ways/Herman's Hermits
   c. Soul & Inspiration/Righteous Brothers

****

2. The band's playing *one of our old favorite songs from way back when.*

   a. Traces/Classics IV
   b. Hello, Dolly/Louis Armstrong
   c. All Summer Long/Beach Boys

****

3. *Just what the truth is,* they *can't say anymore.*

   a. The Sounds of Silence/Simon & Garfunkel
   b. In the Year 2525/Zager & Evans
   c. Nights In White Satin/Moody Blues

****

4. To them, you are as *sweet as roses in the morning* and as *soft as summer rain at dawn.*

   a. Little Girl/Syndicate of Sound
   b. Concrete and Clay/Unit Four Plus Two
   c. You Didn't Have to Be So Nice/Lovin' Spoonful

****

5. *Where are you going with that gun in your hand?*

   a. War/Edwin Starr
   b. Hey Joe/Jimi Hendrix
   c. In the Ghetto/Elvis Presley

ANSWERS

****

1. a. Think/Aretha Franklin
2. b. Glad All Over/Dave Clark Five
3. c. My Girl/Temptations
4. a. Tell It Like It Is/Aaron Neville
5. c. I Think We're Alone Now/Tommy James & the Shondells
6. a. The Tracks of My Tears/Smokey Robinson & the Miracles
7. a. This Is My Song/Petula Clark
8. a. Good Morning Starshine/Oliver
9. c. Piece of My Heart/Big Brother & the Holding Company
10. a. Poor Side of Town/Johnny Rivers
11. b. Hold On I'm Comin'/Sam & Dave
12. c. I'll Follow the Sun/Beatles
13. a. Stoned Soul Picnic/5th Dimension
14. c. Ain't Nothing Like the Real Thing/Marvin Gaye & Tammi Terrell
15. b. Stand By Me/Ben E. King
16. a. I Hear a Symphony/Supremes
17. b. Mustang Sally/Wilson Pickett
18. c. Love Is All Around/Troggs
19. b. I Got You (I Feel Good)/James Brown
20. c. Laugh At Me/Sonny Bono

****

HARDER QUESTIONS--Answers

1. a. The Happening/Supremes
2. b. Hello, Dolly/Louis Armstrong
3. c. Nights In White Satin/Moody Blues
4. b. Concrete and Clay/Unit Four Plus Two
5. b. Hey Joe/Jimi Hendrix

1. *Fire all of your guns at once and explode into space.*
    - a. Time Has Come Today/Chambers Brothers
    - b. Touch Me/Doors
    - c. Born to Be Wild/Steppenwolf

****

2. *No one told* them *about her, though they all knew.*
    - a. Day Tripper/Beatles
    - b. She's Not There/Zombies
    - c. Susan/Buckinghams

****

3. *Blue skies, sunshine — what a day to take a walk in the park.*
    - a. Lazy Day/Spanky & Our Gang
    - b. At the Zoo/Simon & Garfunkel
    - c. Pleasant Valley Sunday/Monkees

****

4. When her soul *was in the lost and found, you came along to claim it.*
    - a. Dream a Little Dream of Me/Mama Cass
    - b. All I See Is You/Dusty Springfield
    - c. (You Make Me Feel Like) A Natural Woman/Aretha Franklin

****

5. *All around there are girls and boys — it's a swinging place, a cellar full of noise.*
    - a. Drag City/Jan & Dean
    - b. Boogaloo Down Broadway/Fantastic Johnny C
    - c. I Know a Place/Petula Clark

6. *Come on without, come on within.*
   a. Journey to the Center of the Mind/Amboy Dukes
   b. The Mighty Quinn (Quinn the Eskimo)/Manfred Mann
   c. Light My Fire/Doors

****

7. They *remember when* they *used to play shoot-em-up bang-bang, baby.*
   a. Oh Happy Days/Edwin Hawkins Singers
   b. Cowboys to Girls/Intruders
   c. Do It Again/Beach Boys

****

8. *It's a pity* that *the days can't be like the nights.*
   a. Summer In the City/Lovin' Spoonful
   b. All Day and All of the Night/Kinks
   c. This Magic Moment/Jay & the Americans

****

9. It's *coming to take you away.*
   a. Magic Carpet Ride/Steppenwolf
   b. Magical Mystery Tour/Beatles
   c. Scarborough Fair/Simon & Garfunkel

****

10. He claims that people are *never meaning what they say* and *never saying what they mean.*
    a. Eve of Destruction/Barry McGuire
    b. Games People Play/Joe South
    c. Simple Song of Freedom/Tim Hardin

11. *You think you're gonna find yourself a little piece of paradise,* but it hasn't happened yet, so *you better think twice.*
   a. Kicks/Paul Revere & The Raiders
   b. White Rabbit/Jefferson Airplane
   c. Mother's Little Helper/Rolling Stones
****

12. *A pretty face you may not possess, but what* they *like about you is your tenderness.*
   a. Beauty Is Only Skin Deep/Temptations
   b. Apples, Peaches, Pumpkin Pie/Jay & the Techniques
   c. She's My Girl/Turtles
****

13. They're not looking *to compete with you, meet or cheat or mistreat you.*
   a. Listen People/Herman's Hermits
   b. All I Really Want to Do/Byrds
   c. Get Together/Youngbloods
****

14. They're *up every morning just to keep* their *job* and they've *got to find* their *way through the hustling mob.*
   a. Dead End Street/Kinks
   b. Pushin' Too Hard/Seeds
   c. Five O'Clock World/Vogues
****

15. *Summer vacation is taking you away.*
   a. Sweet Caroline/Neil Diamond
   b. See You In September/Happenings
   c. Summer Rain/Johnny Rivers

16. *You've got the power to turn on the light.*
    a. Only the Strong Survive/Jerry Butler
    b. Say It Loud—I'm Black and I'm Proud/James Brown
    c. Bend Me, Shape Me/American Breed

****

17. They *had such happiness together* — they *can't believe it's gone forever.*
    a. Yesterday's Gone/Chad & Jeremy
    b. Needles and Pins/Searchers
    c. Don't You Care/Buckinghams

****

18. *Harmony and understanding, sympathy and trust abound it.*
    a. Aquarius—Let the Sunshine In/5th Dimension
    b. Chain of Fools/Aretha Franklin
    c. Sweet Cherry Wine/Tommy James & the Shondells

****

19. *Roses are red* and *all the leaves have gone green.*
    a. Jean/Oliver
    b. Love (Can Make You Happy)/Mercy
    c. My Cherie Amour/Stevie Wonder

****

20. *Falling, yes* they *are falling, and she keeps calling* them *back again.*
    a. Standing In the Shadows of Love/Four Tops
    b. I've Just Seen a Face/Beatles
    c. Eight Miles High/Byrds

HARDER QUESTIONS: Worth 2 points each — 4 points if you can NAME THAT TUNE without the three choices !

****

1. They will do this *even if they live without you.*
   - a. Remember (Walkin' In the Sand)/Shangri-Las
   - b. Sure Gonna Miss Her/Gary Lewis & the Playboys
   - c. I Will Always Think About You/New Colony Six

****

2. She's *old enough to face the dawn.*
   - a. Since You've Been Gone/Aretha Franklin
   - b. Angel of the Morning/Merrilee Rush
   - c. This Is My Song/Petula Clark

****

3. *She strolled on up to* them *and asked, "Hey big boy, what's your name?"*
   - a. Sha La La/Manfred Mann
   - b. Dandelion/Rolling Stones
   - c. She's About A Mover/Sir Douglas Quintet

****

4. *When* they *were young, people spoke of immorality —* but *all the things they said were wrong are what* they *wanted to be.*
   - a. Over Under Sideways Down/Yardbirds
   - b. When I Was Young/Animals
   - c. My Generation/Who

****

5. *Carnivals and cotton candy and you.*
   - a. Love Makes the World Go Round/Deon Jackson
   - b. It's Getting Better/Mama Cass
   - c. Orange Skies/Love

ANSWERS

****

1. c. Born to Be Wild/Steppenwolf
2. b. She's Not There/Zombies
3. a. Lazy Day/Spanky & Our Gang
4. c. (You Make Me Feel Like) A Natural Woman/Aretha Franklin
5. c. I Know a Place/Petula Clark
6. b. The Mighty Quinn (Quinn the Eskimo)/Manfred Mann
7. b. Cowboys to Girls/Intruders
8. a. Summer In the City/Lovin' Spoonful
9. b. Magical Mystery Tour/Beatles
10. b. Games People Play/Joe South
11. a. Kicks/Paul Revere & The Raiders
12. a. Beauty Is Only Skin Deep/Temptations
13. b. All I Really Want to Do/Byrds
14. c. Five O'Clock World/Vogues
15. b. See You In September/Happenings
16. c. Bend Me, Shape Me/American Breed
17. a. Yesterday's Gone/Chad & Jeremy
18. a. Aquarius—Let the Sunshine In/5ᵗʰ Dimension
19. a. Jean/Oliver
20. b. I've Just Seen a Face/Beatles

****

HARDER QUESTIONS--Answers

1. c. I Will Always Think About You/New Colony Six
2. b. Angel of the Morning/Merrilee Rush
3. c. She's About A Mover/Sir Douglas Quintet
4. a. Over Under Sideways Down/Yardbirds
5. c. Orange Skies/Love

1. *Her arms are wicked and her legs are long — when she moves,* their *brain screams out this song.*
   a. Can't Seem to Make You Mine/Seeds
   b. Hello, I Love You/Doors
   c. Rock Me/Steppenwolf

****

2. They've been *for a walk on a winter's day.*
   a. In and Out of Love/Diana Ross & the Supremes
   b. The Sounds of Silence/Simon & Garfunkel
   c. California Dreamin'/The Mamas & the Papas

****

3. People say that they're too young, they don't know and *won't find out until* they *grow.*
   a. I Think We're Alone Now/Tommy James & the Shondells
   b. Daydream Believer/Monkees
   c. I Got You Babe/Sonny & Cher

****

4. They *can't promise that* they'll *spend the day with you* or that they'll *love you.*
   a. Stoned Soul Picnic/5th Dimension
   b. Like to Get to Know You/Spanky & Our Gang
   c. People Got to Be Free/Rascals

****

5. *She didn't know what she was headed for,* and *when she found what she was headed for, it was too late.*
   a. Undun/Guess Who
   b. 1, 2, 3 Red Light/1910 Fruitgum Company
   c. Na Na Hey Hey Kiss Him Goodbye/Steam

6. *Some boys like to run around — they don't think about the things they do — but this boy wants to settle down.*
   a. I Was Made to Love Her/Stevie Wonder
   b. Gimme Little Sign/Brenton Wood
   c. She'd Rather Be With Me/Turtles

****

7. They're *a little bit wrong, you're a little bit right.*
   a. A Little Bit Me, A Little Bit You/Monkees
   b. We Can Work It Out/Beatles
   c. Just a Little/Beau Brummels

****

8. *When you've got nothing, you've got nothing to lose.*
   a. Poor Side of Town/Johnny Rivers
   b. Like a Rolling Stone/Bob Dylan
   c. I'm Free/Who

****

9. The *look in your eyes* was *sweeter than wine* and *softer than a summer night.*
   a. Brown-Eyed Girl/Van Morrison
   b. Devil With a Blue Dress On/Mitch Ryder & the Detroit Wheels
   c. This Magic Moment/Jay & the Americans

****

10. They're *dreaming of your love and not knowing where to start.*
   a. Wild Thing/Troggs
   b. A Groovy Kind of Love/Mindbenders
   c. Everybody Loves a Clown/Gary Lewis & the Playboys

11. He *knows that loves can last for years,* but he wonders *how can love last through tears.*
       a. Ain't That Peculiar/Marvin Gaye
       b. Tell Me Why/Bobby Vinton
       c. I'm Gonna Be Strong/Gene Pitney

****

12. *Some days you will want to cry and some days you will shout.*
       a. Little Bit O' Soul/Music Explosion
       b. Psychotic Reaction/Count Five
       c. This Door Swings Both Ways/Herman's Hermits

****

13. *You don't know what* they're *going through, standing here looking at you.*
       a. I Can't Help Myself/Four Tops
       b. Hurts So Bad/Little Anthony & the Imperials
       c. The Way You Do The Things You Do/Temptations

****

14. *A year has come and gone since* they *heard the news —* and *brother, Mary, Becky Thompson bought a store in Tupelo.*
       a. Love Is Strange/Peaches & Herb
       b. Ode to Billie Joe/Bobbie Gentry
       c. The Beat Goes On/Sonny & Cher

****

15. *His clothes are dirty but his hands are clean,* and *you're the best thing that he's ever seen.*
       a. Lay Lady Lay/Bob Dylan
       b. Mr. Bojangles/Jerry Jeff Walker
       c. When a Man Loves a Woman/Percy Sledge

16. *You can take a cross-town bus if it's raining or it's cold, and the animals will love it if you do.*
    a. England Swings/Roger Miller
    b. At the Zoo/Simon & Garfunkel
    c. MacArthur Park/Richard Harris

    ****

17. *Odds are you won't live to see tomorrow.*
    a. A Boy Named Sue/Johnny Cash
    b. Badge/Cream
    c. Secret Agent Man/Johnny Rivers

    ****

18. *In* their *Woody* they *would take you everywhere* they *go.*
    a. Hang On Sloopy/McCoys
    b. Surfer Girl/Beach Boys
    c. Let's Hang On/Four Seasons

    ****

19. They'd *swim the deepest sea, climb the highest hill* just to have you near them.
    a. I'd Wait a Million Years/Grass Roots
    b. River Deep—Mountain High/Ike & Tina Turner
    c. Standing In the Shadows of Love/Four Tops

    ****

20. *They were the devil's children.*
    a. Ballad of John & Yoko/Beatles
    b. The Ballad of Bonnie and Clyde/Georgie Fame
    c. Creeque Alley/The Mamas & the Papas

HARDER QUESTIONS: Worth 2 points each — 4 points if you can NAME THAT TUNE without the three choices !

****

1. They *tripped on a cloud and fell eight miles high.*
   a. Eight Miles High/Byrds
   b. Just Dropped In (To See What Condition My Condition Was In)/First Edition
   c. Get Me to the World on Time/Electric Prunes

****

2. *Any time you want to, you can turn* them *on to anything you want to anytime at all.*
   a. Itchycoo Park/Small Faces
   b. I'm Your Puppet/James & Bobby Purify
   c. A Groovy Kind of Love/Mindbenders

****

3. *It's been so long.*
   a. Do It Again/Beach Boys
   b. I Got Rhythm/Happenings
   c. Friday On My Mind/Easybeats

****

4. *Sweet soft summer nights, dancing shadows in the starry light.*
   a. Waterloo Sunset/Kinks
   b. Distant Shores/Chad & Jeremy
   c. San Francisco (Be Sure to Wear Some Flowers In Your Hair)/Scott McKenzie

****

5. *You've gone ahead and left* them, *and now the blues they come.*
   a. See See Rider/Animals
   b. Blue Turns to Grey/Rolling Stones
   c. I Go to Pieces/Peter & Gordon

ANSWERS

****

1. b. Hello, I Love You/Doors
2. c. California Dreamin'/The Mamas & the Papas
3. c. I Got You Babe/Sonny & Cher
4. b. Like to Get to Know You/Spanky & Our Gang
5. a. Undun/Guess Who
6. c. She'd Rather Be With Me/Turtles
7. a. A Little Bit Me, A Little Bit You/Monkees
8. b. Like a Rolling Stone/Bob Dylan
9. c. This Magic Moment/Jay & the Americans
10. c. Everybody Loves a Clown/Gary Lewis & the Playboys
11. a. Ain't That Peculiar/Marvin Gaye
12. c. This Door Swings Both Ways/Herman's Hermits
13. b. Hurts So Bad/Little Anthony & the Imperials
14. b. Ode to Billie Joe/Bobbie Gentry
15. a. Lay Lady Lay/Bob Dylan
16. b. At the Zoo/Simon & Garfunkel
17. c. Secret Agent Man/Johnny Rivers
18. b. Surfer Girl/Beach Boys
19. a. I'd Wait a Million Years/Grass Roots
20. b. The Ballad of Bonnie and Clyde/Georgie Fame

****

HARDER QUESTIONS--Answers

1. b. Just Dropped In (To See What Condition My Condition Was In)/First Edition
2. c. A Groovy Kind of Love/Mindbenders
3. a. Do It Again/Beach Boys
4. b. Distant Shores/Chad & Jeremy
5. a. See See Rider/Animals

1. *When your world don't seem just right and life's getting you uptight, you can change that wrong to right.*
   - a. Lady Willpower/Gary Puckett & the Union Gap
   - b. Good Thing/Paul Revere & the Raiders
   - c. Incense and Peppermints/Strawberry Alarm Clock

****

2. He doesn't have time *to think about money and what it can buy.*
   - a. Wichita Lineman/Glen Campbell
   - b. For Once In My Life/Stevie Wonder
   - c. Too Busy Thinking About My Baby/Marvin Gaye

****

3. They feel that *the ice is slowly melting.*
   - a. Sugar Sugar/Archies
   - b. Here Comes The Sun/Beatles
   - c. Hot Fun In the Summertime/Sly & the Family Stone

****

4. They *wonder if you know that you're putting on a show.*
   - a. Hippy Hippy Shake/Swingin' Medallions
   - b. Girl Watcher/O'Kaysions
   - c. I Thank You/Sam & Dave

****

5. The joker said to the thief that "*there must be some kind of way out of here*".
   - a. All Along the Watchtower/Jimi Hendrix
   - b. Release Me/Engelbert Humperdinck
   - c. In-A-Gadda-Da-Vida/Iron Butterfly

6. This is *the worst trip* they've *ever been on.*
   a. Ride Captain Ride/Blues Image
   b. Magic Carpet Ride/Steppenwolf
   c. Sloop John B/Beach Boys

****

7. *Suddenly the sun broke through* — they *turned around* and *she was gone.*
   a. The Rain, The Park and Other Things/Cowsills
   b. I've Gotta Get a Message to You/Bee Gees
   c. I Wonder What She's Doing Tonight/Tommy Boyce & Bobby Hart

****

8. *It makes you feel happy like an old-time movie.*
   a. Do You Believe In Magic/Lovin' Spoonful
   b. Good Morning Starshine/Oliver
   c. Dance to the Music/Sly & the Family Stone

****

9. They *don't hardly know her, but* they *think* they *could love her.*
   a. What Does It Take to Win Your Love/Junior Walker & the All-Stars
   b. These Eyes/Guess Who
   c. Crimson and Clover/Tommy James & the Shondells

****

10. They'll be there *when the day comes and you look down at a river of problems and are about to drown.*
    a. 96 Tears/? & the Mysterians
    b. Little Girl/Syndicate of Sound
    c. Hold On, I'm Comin'/Sam & Dave

11. *Just look over your shoulder,* and they'll *be standing there.*
    a. Reach Out I'll Be There/Four Tops
    b. Monkees Theme (Hey Hey We're the Monkees)/Monkees
    c. Hush/Deep Purple

****

12. Just *like Otis Redding, fa–fa–fa–fa–fa . . . Otis Redding's got the feel of it.*
    a. Classical Gas/Mason Williams
    b. Sweet Soul Music/Arthur Conley
    c. I Got the Feeling/James Brown

****

13. Take their advice and you will see that *you'll be as happy as you can be.*
    a. Take It Or Leave It/Rolling Stones
    b. Good Lovin'/Young Rascals
    c. Listen People/Herman's Hermits

****

14. They *don't know when* they'll *be back again.*
    a. Leaving On a Jet Plane/Peter, Paul & Mary
    b. Journey to the Center of the Mind/Amboy Dukes
    c. Someday We'll Be Together/Diana Ross
       & the Supremes

****

15. *See the tree — how big it's grown.*
    a. Yummy Yummy Yummy/Ohio Express
    b. Honey/Bobby Goldsboro
    c. Only the Strong Survive/Jerry Butler

16. There's a *soft summer breeze and the surf rolls in* as well as the *true laughter of small children playing.*

  a. Turn–Down Day/Cyrkle
  b. Sunshine of Your Love/Cream
  c. A Beautiful Morning/Rascals

****

17. *It's the only thing that there's just too little of.*

  a. Bottle of Wine/Fireballs
  b. What the World Needs Now Is Love/Jackie DeShannon
  c. Green Grass/Gary Lewis & the Playboys

****

18. They were *trying to hitch a ride to San Francisco.*

  a. On the Way Home/Buffalo Springfield
  b. Going Up the Country/Canned Heat
  c. Massachusetts/Bee Gees

****

19. *When* they *start lovin'*, they *can't stop.*

  a. Back Door Man/Doors
  b. Soul Man/Sam & Dave
  c. Jumpin' Jack Flash/Rolling Stones

****

20. *Money feeds* their *music machine.*

  a. Mony Mony/Tommy James & the Shondells
  b. I Can't Stop Dancing/Archie Bell & the Drells
  c. Green Tambourine/Lemon Pipers

HARDER QUESTIONS: Worth 2 points each — 4 points if you can NAME THAT TUNE without the three choices !

****

1. They ask you to *give just a little bit more* and *take a little bit less* and to *love each other tonight.*
   - a. Never Comes the Day/Moody Blues
   - b. Reach Out of the Darkness/Friend & Lover
   - c. Get Together/Youngbloods

****

2. *Roll another one just like the other one . . . c'mon and be a real friend.*
   - a. Stoned Soul Picnic/5th Dimension
   - b. Don't Bogart (That Joint)/Fraternity of Man
   - c. I Want to Take You Higher/Sly & the Family Stone

****

3. *We ain't a-marchin' anymore.*
   - a. Sweet Cherry Wine/Tommy James & the Shondells
   - b. Time Has Come Today/Chambers Brothers
   - c. Simple Song of Freedom/Tim Hardin

****

4. You *don't need no tickets — you just thank the Lord.*
   - a. People Get Ready/Impressions
   - b. Oh Happy Day/Edwin Hawkins Singers
   - c. Yester-Me, Yester-You, Yesterday/Stevie Wonder

****

5. They *never suspected that one of those days the wish of a song would come true.*
   - a. You've Made Me So Very Happy/Blood, Sweat & Tears
   - b. It's You That I Need/Temptations
   - c. Everything That Touches You/Association

ANSWERS

****

1. b. Good Thing/Paul Revere & the Raiders
2. c. Too Busy Thinking About My Baby/Marvin Gaye
3. b. Here Comes The Sun/Beatles
4. b. Girl Watcher/O'Kaysions
5. a. All Along the Watchtower/Jimi Hendrix
6. c. Sloop John B/Beach Boys
7. a. The Rain, The Park and Other Things/Cowsills
8. a. Do You Believe In Magic/Lovin' Spoonful
9. c. Crimson and Clover/Tommy James & the Shondells
10. c. Hold On, I'm Comin'/Sam & Dave
11. b. Monkees Theme (Hey Hey We're the Monkees)/Monkees
12. b. Sweet Soul Music/Arthur Conley
13. c. Listen People/Herman's Hermits
14. a. Leaving On a Jet Plane/Peter, Paul & Mary
15. b. Honey/Bobby Goldsboro
16. a. Turn-Down Day/Cyrkle
17. b. What the World Needs Now Is Love/Jackie DeShannon
18. c. Massachusetts/Bee Gees
19. b. Soul Man/Sam & Dave
20. c. Green Tambourine/Lemon Pipers

****

HARDER QUESTIONS--Answers

1. a. Never Comes the Day/Moody Blues
2. b. Don't Bogart (That Joint)/Fraternity of Man
3. a. Sweet Cherry Wine/Tommy James & the Shondells
4. a. People Get Ready/Impressions
5. c. Everything That Touches You/Association

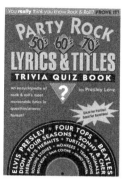

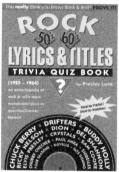

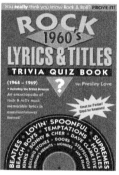

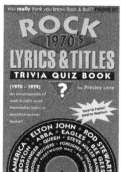

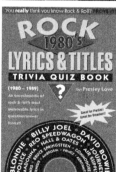

Available on Amazon.com

Printed in Great Britain
by Amazon